BLACK CHILDREN –
WHITE PARENTS

A Study of

Transracial

Adoption

Lucille J. Grow

Deborah Shapiro

Report of a study funded by grant #OCD-CB-59
from Children's Bureau, Office of Child Development, United States Department of Health,
Education and Welfare

Research Center
Child Welfare League of America, Inc.
1974

10/15/82

2nd Printing 1975

Library of Congress Catalog Card Number: 74-29169

ISBN Number: 0-87868-177-9

PREFACE

The need for permanent homes for black children has been a major concern of the Office of Child Development and of the Child Welfare League of America for some time. In 1971 OCD encouraged research and demonstration projects on several aspects of this problem, such as adoption subsidy, aggressive recruitment of black homes, and transracial adoptions. The League's proposed followup study of adoptions of black or part-black children by white parents was funded by the Children's Bureau in the Office of Child Development, and the research reported here was begun.

This study was initiated at about the time when the climate of opinion about transracial adoptions was changing markedly. A decade earlier the adoption of minority group children by white families was generally regarded as a socially desirable way to provide families for children who might otherwise grow up in institutions or in a series of foster homes. Although the Child Welfare League has always stressed the desirability of placing children with families of the same racial or ethnic background, it has also taken the position that a child should not be deprived of a family because of the unavailability of one of the same race. During the early 1960s the League, in cooperation with the Bureau of Indian Affairs, facilitated placement of a number of American Indian children in white adoptive homes.

Similarly, the League has encouraged agencies to consider placing black children in white homes, pending the recruitment of a sufficient number of black adoptive homes.

By the early 1970s, as the maintenance of racial and cultural identity was stressed increasingly by minorities, transracial adoptions came under strong criticism from many quarters. The League was criticized by some for undertaking research on transracial adoptions, which critics regarded as so clearly wrong in principle as to require no study. The League's board shared the opinion of OCD and League staff that this was a social phenomenon meriting examination, whether or not it had had its day by the time the research would be completed. The project certainly generated more emotion and controversy than is usual for our research, but we believe it has been relatively unaffected by these side effects.

How best to evaluate transracial adoptions is a question we may not have answered well, but we did it to the best of our ability. The committee that reviewed our application suggested a comparison group of black children adopted by black families. Serious consideration was given to this, but it was ruled out as unnecessary, since no one had questioned the preferability of within-race adoption if feasible. The question is whether children are better off adopted by parents of a different race than they would be if they lived with neither natural not adoptive parents. To answer that would necessitate following up black children who had been adopted by white parents and children comparable with the adoptees in all respects except that they had not been adopted. Identifying a comparable sample of non-adopted children did not seem possible.

We therefore confined the research to a descriptive study of adoptions of black or part-black children by white parents. We decided to focus on children who were at least 6 years of age so that they would have had some experience in the community, and on children who had been in their adoptive homes at least 3 years, long enough for initial adjustments to be worked out.

Of the 125 children studied, who on the average were about 9 years old and had been in their adoptive homes over 7 years, 77% were judged to represent successful adoptions, a success rate typical of adoption studies, whether of conventional adoptions of white infants by white families or less usual adoptions. So we know the children in our study group appeared to do as well as adopted children in other studies. However, so far as we know, no study has been made of black children adopted by black families.

A major concern in the minds of the critics of transracial adoption is that the child will lose his identification with his racial and cultural heritage. We attempted to explore the child's attitude toward his black heritage, and we treated this variable as one of our outcome measures. We were, however, dependent principally on the parents for information, and we recognize the real possibility of bias on their part. Had we been able to confine the study to adolescents, we might have probed this question more effectively with the adoptees themselves, but we were pessimistic about locating an adequate sample if we set a higher minimum age than we did.

A problem intrinsic to retrospective studies is whether what is being studied is still relevant. Has adoption practice changed since these adoptions were made? Are the characteristics of white adoptive applicants with whom black children are placed comparable with those studied? OCD staff suggested that the League undertake a substudy of current transracial adoptions. That we could locate only 38 cases in the same agencies where we located the sample for the main study clearly indicates one trend in the field--although other agencies have continued to "discover" transracial adoption, the agencies that were in the vanguard in placing black children with white parents have greatly reduced this practice. This substudy, which focuses principally on the adoptive applicant's and the social worker's perceptions, will be reported elsewhere.

The project reported in this book was designed principally by the League's Research Director, in consultation with other League staff. Major responsibility for the operational phase of the research rested with Lucille J. Grow, who was appointed study director. Dr. Grow, who holds a doctorate in sociology, had had long experience in child welfare practice, supervision and research, including several years as Research Associate at the League. In 1973 Deborah Shapiro joined the League's research staff to work with Dr. Grow on data analysis and preparation of this report, and to free some of Dr. Grow's time to launch a new project. Dr. Shapiro, whose doctorate is in social work, also had a substantial background of child welfare experience, including several years as a study director on the Columbia University Child Welfare Research Program.

Two research assistants participated in the project--Diane Engel, who carried responsibility for data control, editing and coding, and Eva Russo, who shepherded the data through the computer. They were important to the research, as was Karen Brown, who has typed seemingly endless data collection schedules and drafts of the report.

The data were gathered by 21 diligent interviewers recruited from the seven areas from which the same was drawn. We would therefore like to thank each of our interviewers, who were:

Sandra Alberg	Gayle McLachlan
Thelma Bell	Michael Meleedy
Ethel Branham	Elaine O'Neal
Nicky Bredeson	Ruth Overocker
Margaret Daughters	Ray Rambally
Patricia Denny	Louise Saltus
Connie Hansen	Bernadette Smetka
Marilyn Horn	Martha Steinmetz
Elizabeth Johnson	Phyllis Vlach
Judy Karon	Nancy Woodfork
Patricia McCullough	

We are also appreciative of the efforts of the following agencies in identifying from their files cases that fit our study criteria and in obtaining permission from the adoptive parents to refer them to us:

Boston
Area
Boston Children's Service Association
Catholic Charitable Bureau of Boston, Inc.
Commonwealth of Massachusetts, Department
    of Public Welfare
Jewish Family and Children's Service
New England Home for Little Wanderers

Chicago
Area
Catholic Charities of the Archdiocese
    of Chicago
Chicago Foundlings Home
Illinois Children's Home and Aid Society
Lake Bluff/Chicago Homes for Children
Lutheran Welfare Services of Illinois

Los Angeles
Area
County of Los Angeles, Department of
    Adoptions

Detroit
Area
Catholic Social Services of Washtenaw County
Child and Family Services of Michigan, Inc.
Lutheran Children's Friend Society of Michigan
Washtenaw County Department of Social Services

Minneapolis-
St. Paul
Area
Children's Home Society
Hennepin County Welfare Department
Lutheran Social Service of Minnesota
Social Services Division, County Welfare
    Department, City of St. Paul and County of
    Ramsey

Montreal
Area
Children's Service Centre

Seattle
Area

Catholic Children's Services
Children's Home Society of Washington
State of Washington, Department
   of Social and Health Services
Lutheran Family and Child Service of
   Washington
Medina Children's Service

Finally, we would like to extend special thanks to the

parents, the children and the teachers who supplied the informa-

tion that makes this report possible, but who must remain anony-

mous.

Ann W. Shyne
Director of Research

CONTENTS

Chapter 1

INTRODUCTION

Adoption by white families of children of black or part-
black parentage began in the early 1950s and increased in volume
during the 1960s, with increasing numbers of agencies making
transracial adoptive placements. Despite the growth of this
phenomenon over more than two decades, relatively little systema-
tic study has been made of the outcome of such adoptions.

Although there are no hard data on the total number of black
children placed transracially, surveys conducted by the Boys and
Girls Aid Society of Oregon show that for the 260 agencies on
which trend data were available between 1969 and 1971 there was
a 40% increase in the number of black children placed in white
homes.[1] A variety of societal forces have accounted for the
increase in the placement of children across racial lines.

Factors Contributing to Transracial Adoptions

Increasing Visibility of Black Children in Need of Substitute Care

The need for permanent substitute homes for black children
has long been a critical problem in child welfare. Many black

---

1. "Adoption of Black Children in 1971," Opportunity, issued by
the Boys and Girls Aid Society of Oregon.

children have spent their childhood moving from one impermanent living arrangement to another. Many of the black children who are admitted to the social welfare system spend their childhood years in institutions and foster homes.

As the civil rights movement gained momentum, however, agencies were prompted to give more attention to the plight of the black child. Discriminatory practices that resulted in differential plans being made for white and black children began to be examined more closely. Questions began to be raised about the long-accepted assumption that cultural differences were the reason black unwed mothers tended to keep their children, whereas white unwed mothers usually relinquished their children for adoption. Although these questions have not yet been laid to rest, examination of agency policies and practices indicated that some of the options available to the white unwed mother were not available to the black unwed mother.

Agencies heretofore engaged primarily in the placement of white children in white adoptive homes began to concern themselves with adoptive placement of those black children under their care. Some agencies that had previously restricted intake mainly to white children began to admit black children on the basis of need rather than on the basis of the then-available agency resources.

In many instances agency policies were modified to attract more black adoptive applicants, but since they did not attract enough black applicants for the children in need of permanent homes, some agencies began to experiment with transracial adoption. This was consonant with the attitude prevailing during the early phases of the civil rights movement--that racial integration was the desirable route to full participation of blacks in American society. It is of interest that not only white adoption workers were involved in this early movement. Some black adoption workers, concerned with the plight of the black children in their caseloads, saw this as a perhaps less-preferable but nevertheless pragmatic means of giving black children the kind of continuing care, nurturance and sense of belonging so important to the child's optimum physical, emotional and social development.

Decrease in Adoptable White Infants

Particularly during the latter part of the 1960s, agencies began to experience a decrease in the number of white unwed mothers who were giving up their children for adoptive placement. The availability of contraception and abortion reduced the number of unwanted children. The changing social climate, with less stigma attached to women who became pregnant out of wedlock, made it more acceptable than in the past for these mothers to keep their children. Adoption programs in voluntary agencies, often reliant upon adoption fees for much of their income, had more white adoptive applicants than healthy white infants available. Some agencies phased out their adoption services completely, and others reduced their staff. Many agencies changed their focus to adoptive placement of children with special needs--the handicapped, the older child, sibling groups and the minority child.

The Population Explosion and the Media

During the 1960s the problem of an excess of people to natural resources began to gain more and more publicity. It was no longer stylish to have large families. Indeed, it was not social-minded. The pill and other methods of contraception made it easier to plan one's family. Many couples chose not to have children or to have only one or two.

On the other hand, many couples who had decided on restricting childbirth to a very few children or none, nevertheless were interested in parenting or in expanding their families through adoption. The mass media--newspapers, magazines, and television in particular--were bringing to the public not only the plight of children in need of permanent care, but also the "success" stories of couples who had adopted children with special needs. Possibly because many of these couples knew that they could reproduce if they so desired, the adoption of a child who might always stand out as very different in appearance from them held less of a threat to them than it had to many adoptive applicants in the past.

Study Design

Purpose of the Study

Information about the outcome of transracial adoptions and about the circumstances associated with greater or lesser well-being of the child is important to agencies in planning for children and in providing appropriate services to adoptive parents. The Child Welfare League of America undertook the study reported here in order to obtain such information.

As we have said, at the time this study was conceived there was an increasing trend among adoption agencies to place children across racial lines. Simultaneously with the launching, of the study, previously muted voices against transracial adoption began to rise to a crescendo. In the spring of 1972, at its first annual convention, the National Association of Black Social Workers expressed its "vehement opposition to the practice of placing black children with white families."[2] At the behest of the Urban League, the Child Welfare League had included, in the 1968 edition of its adoption standards, the statement that "racial background in itself should not determine the selection of a home for a child";[3] however, its 1973 revised standards, while recognizing transracial adoption as one means of providing permanent homes for children, also states: "In today's social climate, children placed in adoptive families with similar racial characteristics can become more easily integrated into the average family group and community."[4]

This study was undertaken at a time when the tide was obviously changing. "Transracial adoptions can't work" is now the byword among many blacks, and very likely among many whites as well. Whether there are numerically fewer black children being placed in

2. New York Times, April 10, 1972.

3. CWIA Standards for Adoption Service. New York: Child Welfare League of America, 1968, p. 25.

4. CWIA Standards for Adoption Service. New York: Child Welfare League of America, revised 1973, p. 92.

white homes today is not known. What is known is that most of the agencies that pioneered in transracial adoption are making fewer and fewer of these placements.

Although there has been a number of studies, usually of recent adoptions and confined to a single locale, the data on the outcome of black-white cross-racial adoptions have been sparse. This is particularly true in relation to the school-age child and to the child who has been with the adoptive family for some time. How are these children getting along in the home, in the school and in the community at large? What are the attitudes of these children toward their racial background? Are there any child, family or community characteristics that can be identified with successful outcome?

The findings of this study can tell us something about how these families were faring at the time they were interviewed. They can give us clues as to the characteristics of parents, child and surrounding environment that have tended to make for more or less successful outcomes. Since the social scene continues to change, how much these findings are relevant to children placed trans-racially today is moot.

Population From Which the Study Group Was Drawn

The study is a followup of black children who were at least 6 years of age by January 1, 1972, and who had been in their white adoptive homes for at least 3 years by that date. In instances of families who had adopted more than one black child, the oldest child was selected for the study.

The plan called for interviewing the families at the point when they were identified and again a year later. The purpose of the second interview was to correct for any transient effects and to obtain some hint of whether outcomes over time are relatively stable or tend to shift in a positive or negative direction.

An early question to be resolved was the pool from which the subjects would be drawn. One option would have been to advertise in local newspapers for willing subjects. Aside from the question of representativeness, this would have been a costly and cumbersome procedure, both in money and time, with the inevitable necessity of weeding out ineligibles. A second option was to enlist the cooperation of the many adoptive parent groups that have sprung up throughout the country. Two reasons militated against this. For one thing, adoptive parents who are active in these groups may be markedly different from those who are not, and therefore not representative of transracially adopting parents in general. The second reason stemmed from our interest in including as many older children as possible in the study, particularly children who had been in the adoptive home a substantial number of years. Since in many locales these adoptive parent groups have emerged only within the last few years, it seemed highly unlikely that families who had adopted many years earlier would be active in them.[5]

---

5. Indeed, in the course of interviewing in one locale where an adoptive parent group had been organized about 5 years previously, it turned out that few, if any, of those interviewed had been aware of this group.

The third option, and the one finally decided upon, was to enlist the support of social agencies in communities in which a sizable number of black children had been placed in white adoptive homes. Since the families had been assured of confidentiality at the time of the adoption, the initial approach to these families to ask their participation had to be made through the social agency. Obviously, this method of obtaining our study population has drawbacks. The study is confined to children placed by social agencies, and to families who responded to the agencies' requests for their participation. We have no way of knowing how different those families who were not reached or who refused to participate are from those who did agree to do so.

Identification of Communities in Which the Study Would Be Conducted

To keep the field operation manageable, we tried to locate clusters of children who met the criteria in a limited number of areas, but in areas that are diversified geographically and in type of community. Data collected by the Boys and Girls Aid Society of Oregon on transracial placements enabled us to identify approximately 15 localities with substantial numbers of black children placed in white adoptive homes in 1970. Letters describing the project were sent to about 70 agencies in these areas. The letters generally elicited a positive interest in the research. In most instances, however, the agencies reported having few, if any, black children who were 6 years of age and who had been in their white adoptive homes for at least 3 years. There were also a few agencies with substantial experience with transracial placements

-8-

that were unable to identify possible research subjects, since the race of neither the child nor the adoptive parents was indicated in their records.

Further correspondence resulted in the selection of seven areas: Boston, Chicago, Detroit, Los Angeles, Minneapolis-St. Paul, Montreal and Seattle. To enlist cooperation, in all of the communities except Los Angeles and Montreal--in each of which a single agency had a substantial number of eligible cases--meetings were held with every voluntary and public agency that might have eligible cases. In all, 25 agencies were involved in this early effort, although ultimately only 22 were successful in obtaining consents from eligible families. In each of the 22 agencies one person was designated as liaison and was responsible for trans-mitting information to one of the interviewers regarding those families who had agreed to participate.

In the preliminary contacts with the potential agency parti-cipants we had asked for an estimate of the number of families each agency had who would meet the criteria for inclusion in the study. The selection of the seven participating communities was based on these estimates. Not surprisingly, but disappointingly, their estimate of 281 eligible families was considerably in excess (19%) of the actual number found to be eligible--227 families. In many instances agencies had not kept separate statistics by race of adoptive family and of child, and, when the case record was examined, it was found that the adoptive parents were black or that the child's racial background was other than black. In some

instances the child did not meet the age requirement, and in other
instances there was duplicate reporting of a family that had
adopted more than one child.

As soon as the eligible families were identified, the agency
sent a standard letter to the last known address of the family,
describing the purpose of the study and requesting the family's
permission to have a research interviewer get in touch with them
to arrange an interview. If the family did not respond to the
initial agency letter or if the letter was returned, the agency
was asked to take additional steps to reach the family. In some
instances a phone call was made; in others a letter was sent
requesting the family's forwarding address. Aggressive efforts
to locate nonrespondents were not usually undertaken by the
agencies. Upon a family's affirmative response, the agencies
furnished to a research interviewer the information needed to
locate the family.

Of the 227 families finally identified by the agencies as
eligible, it was not possible to locate 43, or approximately a
fifth. (Table 1-1) Since the letters sent with forwarding
addresses requested were returned to the agency, it is likely
that these families had moved more than once since the adoption
was legalized.

Of those located, 59 could not be interviewed. In 13 instances
the families had moved to an area so distant from any of the seven
locales in which the research interviewers were based that, despite
the family's agreement to participate in many cases, the travel

expense would have been too costly. There were 12 outright refusals and an additional 32 implicit refusals in which the families did not return the consent-to-be-interviewed forms sent to them by the agency. The two remaining families agreed to be interviewed but the research interviewer was unable to reach them to make an appointment prior to the cut-off date for interviewing.

Table 1-1

Outcome of Attempt to Obtain Initial Interviews

	No.	%
Unable to locate family	43	19
Located, but geographically inaccessible	13	6
Family did not return consent	32	14
Outright refusal	12	5
Permission given, but interview not obtained	2	1
Parent interview obtained	125	55
Total	227	100

In all, interviews were conducted with 125 families--approximately three-fourths (73%) of the 171 families located within a reasonable radius of one of the seven communities. With 10 exceptions, the 125 families lived within 100 miles of one of these communities.

It took slightly more than 7 months--from February 13, 1972, until September 22, 1972--to complete the first round of interviewing.

The second interviews, conducted approximately a year later, were
spread out over an 8-month period, from February 3, 1973, to
October 8, 1973.

Data Collection

The first in-person contact, averaging about 3-3/4 hours,
consisted of a joint parent interview, individual interviews with
the parents, and administration of the California Test of
Personality to the child. In the joint parent interview inquiry
was made into the general family situation, the neighborhood, the
family's leisure time activities, the study child's behavior and
adjustment, the adoption experience, the adoptive parents' contacts
with blacks and black culture, and their general satisfaction or
dissatisfaction with the adoption. With two exceptions, the
interviews were conducted in the family's home.

Immediately following this joint parent interview, each parent
was interviewed separately while the other parent completed a
questionnaire. The individual parent interview was directed toward
exploring the reaction of family and friends to the adoption, the
parent's relationship to and activities with the child, and the
parent's own feelings about the adoption. The parent questionnaire
inquired into attitudes about childrearing and the types of "waiting"
children the parent would have considered adopting. It also included
the Weinstein Scale of Well-being[6] as well as several scales from

6. Eugene A. Weinstein, The Self-Image of the Foster Child. New
    York: Russell Sage Foundation, 1960.

the Missouri Children's Behavior Checklist[7] on which the parent
was asked to rate the child.

During the early planning stage considerable thought had been
given to whether it would be feasible to obtain information directly
from the child. Several approaches were considered. Some instruments or measurement devices could not have been employed without
considerable additional expense; others would be appropriate only
to children within a specified age range. A semistructured interview with the child might have elicited rich data; on the other
hand, interviewers who may readily establish rapport with a latency-
age child might have great difficulty with an adolescent, and vice
versa. It was therefore concluded that a standardized test would
be more productive and might be more acceptable to the parents.
With the parents' permission, the California Test of Personality
was administered to the child to obtain an assessment of the child's
personal and social adjustment.

Following termination of the interview, the research interviewer completed a form reporting on her or his observations of
the family. The interviewer was asked to rate the family on such
matters as the relationship of the parents to each other and to the
child, the attitude of the parents toward the interviewer, and the
estimated reliability of the information obtained.

7. Jacob O. Sines et al., "Identification of Clinically Relevant
    Dimensions of Children's Behavior," Journal of Consulting and
    Clinical Psychology, 33 (1969), 728-734.

During this first contact, the interviewer sought the parents' permission to request information about the child from one other source--the child's school teacher. If the parents' permission was obtained, the interviewer mailed a one-page form to the teacher, requesting the teacher's judgment about the child's academic work and about selected aspects of the child's behavior in and out of the classroom as compared with the academic work and behavior of the child's classmates. In addition, the teacher was asked to assess the child's well-being on the Weinstein Scale, also included in the parent questionnaire.

The second contact with the family, occurring about a year later, was somewhat shorter. Whenever possible, the parents were again interviewed jointly. This interview focused mainly on the general family situation during the preceding year, the neighborhood in which the family was living, and the behavior, adjustment, racial awareness and sense of identity of the child.

At the conclusion of the interview, each parent was asked to complete a questionnaire that contained 35 Likert-type statements pertaining to transracial adoption and to attitudes toward blacks. Four possible types of white-black adoptions were also presented (e.g., adoption by black families of children both of whose parents are white; adoption by white families of children one of whose parents is black) and the parent was asked to specify which types should be encouraged or discouraged. In addition to completing two sentences pertaining to transracial adoption, the parents again were requested to rate their child on the Weinstein Scale of Well-being.

The interviewers completed a one-page form reporting their impressions of the family. These included observations on the marital relationship, each parent's relationship to the child, the child's skin coloring and features, the degree to which each parent acknowledged the child's blackness, the parent's feeling tone when responding to racial differences, the interviewer's impression of how well the adoption had worked out to date, and the estimated reliability of the information obtained in the interview.

At Time 1 (the initial contact), 125 joint parent interview schedules were administered. The mother was always present for the joint parent interview and, except where there was no father in the home, the father usually was present also. All of the mothers and 114 fathers completed the parent questionnaire and participated in the individual parent interview. In 10 instances there was no father present in the home and in one instance the marriage was so recent that the father was reluctant to become involved. (Table 1-2)

The California Test of Personality was administered to 113 of the children. There were seven refusals—five by parents and two by the children themselves. The other five children were either temporarily or, in one instance, permanently absent from the home at the time of the interviewer's visit.

Table 1-2

Schedules Completed at Time 1 and Time 2

Schedules Completed	Time 1	Time 2
Joint Parent Interview	125	114
Individual Parent Interview		
Mother	125	N.A.*
Father	114	N.A.
Parent Questionnaire		
Mother	125	112
Father	114	105
California Test of Personality	113	N.A.
School Report Form	92	N.A.
Interviewer Form	125	114

*Not applicable

Permission to contact the school was obtained on 108 children, but only 92 teachers returned the forms. In 12 instances, parents refused permission for information to be obtained from the child's teacher. In some of these cases the parents indicated that there was a conflict currently between teacher and pupil, and they did not wish to place their child in further jeopardy. It was not possible to obtain information from the teacher on five other children, because there had been a change in teachers, the school was in summer recess, or the child was in college or else was no longer attending school.

A year later (Time 2) the joint parent interview schedule was administered to 114 of the 125 families. Parent questionnaires were obtained from 112 mothers and 105 fathers. Except in three cases, the discrepancy between the number of joint parent interview schedules and the number of parent questionnaires completed is due to the family's being incomplete--that is, there was only one parent living in the home.

Although we had hoped to reinterview all the families seen at Time 1, for a variety of reasons this was not possible or feasible. In one instance in which the adopted child had left the home prior to the Time 1 interview, there was little point in reinterviewing the family. All members of another of the families except the adoptive father were killed in a plane crash. Of the remaining nine families, two were living abroad throughout the second phase of the interviewing, and two had moved and could not be located. The illness of an interviewer just prior to the cut-off date accounted for the loss of second interviews with two other families. The three remaining families, including one in which the adopted child is severely and irreversibly handicapped due to an accident, refused to be interviewed a second time--a refusal rate of about 2%.

An analysis was undertaken of the characteristics of the 114 families who participated in the second interview and the 11 families who did not. Fifty-three variables pertaining to the family and the child, the parents' motivation in adopting and their handling of matters concerning the child's adoption and racial background, as well as the child's adjustment as indicated by the parents, the teacher and the California Test of Personality, were examined. Statistically significant differences at the .05 and .02 level, respectively, were found on two of these variables. Those families who were seen at Time 2 tended to have been more open in discussing their child's racial background. A smaller proportion of the mothers who participated in both the Time 1 and Time 2 interviews than of those seen only at Time 1 saw the adoption as having worked out less well than they had anticipated.

The Interviewers

In each community part-time interviewers were hired to conduct the interviews with the adoptive families. With the exception of one community in which there turned out to be only a handful of families to be interviewed, two or three interviewers were assigned to the project in each locale. All of the interviewers had had experience in social work and the majority had Master's Degrees.

One interviewer in each community was assigned responsibility for allocation of interview assignments, for distribution to interviewers of appropriate schedules, and for local liaison with the participating agencies. During the course of the study, 21 interviewers participated in the followup. Two of the 17 interviewers initially hired resigned because of a family move and had to be replaced, and two additional interviewers were needed to cover the work.

Prior to the Time 1 and the Time 2 interviews, training sessions were held with the interviewers in each locale. The schedules were reviewed and role-playing was utilized to familiarize the interviewers with the schedules and to clarify any ambiguities.

On the whole the interviewers were deeply involved in the project, were enthusiastic about sharing their experiences with the project director, and offered valuable clues in regard to areas that might be covered in the second interviews with the families. Many of the interviewers had had experience in placing children transracially and viewed their contacts with these families as a learning experience.

In the early planning stages considerable thought and discussion had been given to the question of the interviewer's race. Would it be better to have black interviewers, white interviewers or a combination of both? Would white parents be less likely to discuss any race-related problems of their children with a black interviewer? Would a white interviewer be less likely to pick up possible racist attitudes than a black interviewer?

Not unexpectedly, there was no consensus. Some blacks favored using only black interviewers; others thought it didn't matter. Similarly, whites had differing opinions. Our compromise was to try to hire at least one black interviewer in each community. However, since we relied on local social agencies to suggest social workers and since in many instances there were few black social workers in a community, we succeeded in employing black interviewers in only four of the seven communities. Of the 18 who interviewed at Time 1, 13 were white, and of the 19 who interviewed at Time 2, 14 were white.

On 10 variables, seven for Time 1 and three for Time 2, the cases assigned to black and to white interviewers showed statistically significant differences. These variables are:

Racial composition of neighborhood (.01)
Having black friends or neighbors prior to the
    adoption (.05)
Child's attitude toward her/his black heritage (.01)
Child's awareness of racial background (.02)
Racial background of child's friends (.05)
Race of child's close classmates (.05)
Anticipation of difficulties due to child's
    black background (.05)
Child's experience of cruelty from others
    because of black background (.05)
Father's satisfactions in adopting transracially (.02)
Father's initial reaction to interviewer (.01)

The parents seen by white interviewers more frequently described their neighborhoods as all white, less often reported that
prior to this adoption they had black friends or neighbors, and
more often indicated that the child had only white friends and
close classmates. It may be that parents felt more free to give
these responses to white interviewers. On the other hand, interviewers were assigned clusters of families preferably in areas
convenient to their own homes. These differences could conceivably
be a function of the method of assignment.

Other differences between the responses given to white and
black interviewers seem less likely to be a function of interview
assignments. Parents reported more frequently to black than white
interviewers that their child did not know of her or his black
background and that they did not anticipate that their child would
have special difficulties due to race. In contrast to reports to
white interviewers of positive or negative attitudes, black interviewers were more frequently told that the child's attitude toward
her or his black heritage was either one of not knowing or one of

not caring. It may be that issues concerning the child's race created discomfort and ensuing denial for parents having black interviewers. Further substantiation for this explanation is the finding that a larger proportion of parents seen by white than by black interviewers reported that their children had been called names or had been subjected to other types of cruelty from their classmates or playmates because of their racial background.

No differences were found between the responses of mothers seen by white and by black interviewers on the special satisfaction they had derived in adopting transracially. However, a far greater proportion of fathers told white interviewers of the benefit to themselves and to their families through becoming less prejudiced, increasing their understanding, enriching their homes, etc., while the responses given to the black interviewers more frequently reflected satisfaction from helping others (the children themselves or society in general), or no special satisfaction in adopting transracially.

The one other variable that yielded a statistically significant difference between cases assigned to black and to white interviewers was the interviewers' evaluation of the adoptive fathers' initial reaction to them. Whereas white interviewers tended to rate the fathers as somewhat cooperative, black interviewers were more likely to rate them as very highly cooperative. No such differences were found in the rating of the adoptive mothers.

Some of the differences in responses to white and black interviewers may be attributed to chance, and some may be a function of the method of assignment. On the other hand, there may be something in the interaction that results in different responses to some items, depending on whether the interviewer is white or black.

Coding Operations and Statistical Analysis of Data

Manuals were developed for coding of the data. All interviews were coded twice to insure reliability. Where discrepancies were found in the coding, the project director met with the two coders, and a final decision was made at that time. The discrepancies usually occurred in coding responses to open-ended questions and responses by the adoptive parents that appeared to contradict information they had given previously.

The data were punched on IBM cards and the punching was verified. Prior to data analysis, the data for both Time 1 and Time 2 were checked for internal consistency, 25 variables being used in Time 1 and 22 in Time 2.

Data analysis included correlational analysis that served two purposes. It was used to develop a series of indices reflecting forms of outcome that could be used to measure the relative success of the adoptive placements. It also served to combine related variables to form indices that reflect a variety of attitudes considered relevant to the success of transracial adoptions. The content of each index is described in subsequent chapters.

The outcome measures are described in detail in Chapter 4. The mean of all the outcome measures obtained was computed in each case and used as a summary measure of success. This summary

measure and each form of outcome was cross-tabulated against 55
independent variables, which included demographic characteristics
of the child and the family, characteristics of the adoption
experience, aspects of the family's life style, their attitudes
toward racial issues, and characteristics of the community in
which they lived.

For those outcomes on which differences statistically significant at or beyond the .10 level were found on a number of
variables, a regression analysis was done to assess the relative
influence of these variables and determine whether each accounted
for a statistically significant degree of variance, even when the
other variables were controlled. Chapters 5-9 present the findings
with respect to each of the outcome measures.

Since a review of the interview data suggested the presence
in the sample of two distinguishably different groups of adoptive
families, a cluster analysis was done that supported this inference.
Accordingly each family was placed in one of the two categories in
the typology demonstrated, and differences between the two groups
in relation to the outcome and the attitudinal measures were
explored by cross-tabulation. The typology is discussed in detail
in Chapter 10.

Chapter 2

THE CHILDREN AND THEIR ADOPTIVE FAMILIES

In this chapter we present descriptive data on the children and their adoptive families. Some of the information was obtained during the first interview with the 125 families, and some during the second interview, when the study population was slightly smaller. Since in most respects the families not seen at Time 2 are similar to those who were seen, for ease of reading the data will usually be presented as descriptive of the total initial study population.

The Children

The initial study group consisted of 61 girls and 64 boys. At the time that most of the children entered their current homes, adoption had been the plan. However, there were 16 children who had initially entered their homes as foster children, without a plan for adoption.

At the time of the first interview, the children had been living with their adoptive parents anywhere from 2 years and 10 months to slightly over 18 years, with the bulk of them (62%) having been with these families between 5 and 9 years. The median length of time was 7.2 years. The children ranged in age from 5 years 7 months to slightly over 19 years, and 84, or two-thirds, of them were under 10. Their median age was 8.8 years.

Table 2-1

Length of Time in Adoptive Home, by Age,
at Time of First Interview

Time in Adoptive Home	Age Under 8 (N=48) %	8-9 (N=36) %	10-11 (N=21) %	12 & Over (N=20) %	Total (N=125) %
Under 5 years (N=19)	23	11	9	10	15
5-6 (N=39)	62	17	14	-	31
7-8 (N=38)	15	67	29	5	31
9+ (N=29)	-	5	48	85	23
Total	100	100	100	100	100

As is apparent from Table 2-1 and as would be expected, length of time in the adoptive home is associated with age, but the pattern is not entirely consistent. For example, 10% of the children 12 years of age and older had been in their adoptive homes less than 5 years.

Not surprisingly, on the average the study children were older when placed than is usually the case for adoptions in general. Of the children reported as adopted in the United States by unrelated persons through agencies in the years from 1964 to 1970, from 52% to 63% were under 3 months of age at time of placement, while only 13% to 19% were 1 year or older.[1]

1. Children's Bureau Statistical Series 88. U.S. Department of Health, Education and Welfare. Annual reports on adoptions.

For our study group the proportions were reversed, with only 14% of the children placed before 3 months of age and 57% at least a year old when placed. The median age at placement was 13.9 months. (Table 2-2) Indeed, one child was over $9\frac{1}{2}$ years old when she entered the adoptive home.

Table 2-2

Age of Children at Placement

	No.	%
Under 3 months	18	14
3 - 5	12	10
6 - 11	24	19
12 - 17	26	21
18 - 35	25	20
36 months and over	20	16
Total	125	100
Median	13.9 months	

With three exceptions, at the time of followup the children were living with one or both parents--10 with mother only, 111 with both adoptive parents, and one with the adoptive mother and her new spouse. One child, who was described as being emotionally disturbed at the time he entered the adoptive home, had been placed in a residential treatment center several months prior to the first interview, but was back living with the parents at Time 2. In another situation, the family had joined a commune; at both Time 1 and Time 2 the child, with whom the parents had frequent contact, was living separately with a peer group. A third youngster, who maintained sporadic contact with

her family, had left home to live on her own about 2 years prior
to the first interview. Since at Time 2 she was still living
on her own and the parents had had little or no contact with
her, no attempt was made to reinterview them.

Information about the children's biological parents was
limited to that provided by the adoptive parents. Although it
may be subject to some bias, from the project director's experience in reviewing case records in general in which information is frequently contradictory or unclear, it would seem that
the data provided by the adoptive parents may be as reliable as
that available in the case records. Both parents of 15 children (12% of the 125) are reported to be black, and 103 children (82%) are reported to have one black parent. In the remaining seven cases the adoptive parents had no information
about whether both or even one of their child's biological
parents were black.

Although the vast majority (90%) of the children are
described by the parents as having fair or light brown skin
coloring, over 60% of all the children are said to have some
Negroid features. According to the parents, however, for only
slightly more than half the children (55%) is the fact of the
child's being black obvious to others.

The School Situation

As might be expected from their age distribution, the
school grade placement of these children at Time 1 ranged from

kindergarten (6 children) to college (1). Seven children were in an ungraded class or "open classroom." Only one child, a 17-year old youngster no longer living with her adoptive family, was not attending school. Most of the children (83%) were in public school. Less than a tenth (9%) attended a private school, 5% were in parochial school, and the remaining few (3%) were attending special schools for the emotionally disturbed or the handicapped.

The staffing of the schools that the children were attending was predominantly white. Less than a third (31%) of the schools employed any black teachers, and about half of these schools usually had only one or "a few" black teachers on staff. Although a tenth (11%) of the children had had a black teacher at some time, only two children had black teachers at the time of the study. Only a tenth of the children were attending all-white schools, but about two-fifths of the children were the only nonwhites in the classroom, and nearly two-thirds had no black classmates.

For three-fifths of these children one or both parents rated the child's intelligence from superior to very superior, and only 6% of the children were rated as below average. Although at some point in their schooling 2% of the children had skipped a grade and 8% had repeated a grade, for the vast majority school progression had been normal. At Time 1 half the children (51%) were described by their parents as doing above average or excellently in school and over a third (35%) were said to be doing at least average work, with only 14% reported as performing below average. At Time 2 a slightly smaller proportion were described as above average, and a slightly larger proportion as average, but the proportion below average was almost the same.

The parents' assessment of the child's academic work correlated positively with the teachers' reports for the children for whom both assessments were available, but the teachers tended to rate the children somewhat lower. Well over two-fifths were rated by their teachers as above average in comparison with the academic work of their classroom peers, but a fifth were rated as below average. (Table 2-3)

Table 2-3

Teacher Evaluation of Study Child as Compared with
Other Children in Class

	Above Average %	Average %	Below Average %	Number Reported on Item
Academic work	44	35	21	91
Interest in work	48	40	12	92
Curiosity, motiviation to learn	48	38	14	92
Creativity	43	45	12	91
Classroom behavior	39	41	20	91
Behavior during recess	35	51	14	88
Relations with classmates	40	54	6	91
Relations with teachers	48	47	5	92

As may be seen from Table 2-3, the teachers' ratings indicate that on the whole these children are doing well in school. Almost half were rated above average in their interest in school work, their intellectual curiosity and their relations with the teacher. Classroom and recess behavior were the only items on which less than two-fifths of the children were rated above average.

The teachers were also requested to rate the child on the Weinstein Scale of Well-Being, indicating how well the child is likely to get along in life. The teacher was to check one of seven statements, ranging from "Will be able to handle anything. Will make out fine regardless of the situation" to "Will have difficulty in weathering anything but the simplest type of situation. Will need constant protection in even ordinary life situations." In this instance the comparison was not restricted to the child's classroom peers. It is perhaps for this reason that the ratings were somewhat less positive than those on school performance. Although well over two-fifths of the children were rated as above average in their ability to cope with life's problems, almost a fourth were believed to be somewhat less capable of problem-coping than the average child, with half of these in need of a supporting environment at all times.

According to the parents, about a third of the children had misbehaved at some point during their school career to the extent that this misbehavior was reported to the parents. The

incidents ranged from acting-out behavior such as smoking, tru-
ancy, sassiness and disobedience, to internalized symptoms such
as passivity and withdrawal. The most frequent complaints concerned the child's being disruptive in class and seeking attention. For about half the children reported, the problem no
longer existed and for almost a fifth the parents were unaware
whether or not their child was still misbehaving.

In the interval between the first and second interview, 16%
of the children were reported to their parents because of behavior problems. A few children (three) were not promoted or
else had to go to summer school for make-up classes. On the
other hand, 20% of the children received special recognition in
awards for their intellectual ability or for their accomplish-
ments in sports, music or the area of "good citizenship."

The Children's Health

With few exceptions the children were reported in good
health and symptom-free. At Time 1 all but four of the children were considered to be in good health, and in only three
instances had illness interfered at all with the child's daily
routine. When asked to compare the study child's health with
the health of other children in the family, the parents described the health of about three-fourths of the children as no
different from that of their siblings, (i.e., other children in
the adoptive home), while 3% were considered to be in better
health and 8% in worse health. The rest were better or worse

than some but not all of the other children in the home.

During the course of both interviews with the parents they were given a list of 12 somatic complaints or symptoms and asked in each instance whether the symptom was often, seldom, sometimes or not at all true for their child. With the exception of unusual restlessness, which was reported at Time 1 as sometimes or often true for 31% of the children, and nailbiting, for 21%, less than a fifth of the children were reported as sometimes or often having any of the complaints. (Table 2-4) The responses at Time 1 and Time 2 were similar, with the exception of a decrease in reported frequency of colds and of bad dreams or nightmares.

Table 2-4

Somatic Symptoms or Complaints

125 Children--Time 1

Symptom or Complaint	Not at All %	Seldom %	Sometimes %	Often %
Not hungry at mealtime	68	14	12	6
Catches colds easily	47	36	10	7
Bites fingernails	73	6	14	7
Eyes hurt	90	6	2	2
Has sneezing spells	92	2	4	2
Sucks thumb	85	5	5	5
Is unusually restless	62	7	17	14
Has headaches	77	15	7	1
Is tired in morning	81	6	10	3
Wets bed	77	7	5	11
Feels sick at school	76	14	10	--
Bad dreams or nightmares	71	12	14	3

A somatic symptom score was developed by assigning 1 point to the response "seldom," 2 points to "sometimes," and 3 points to "often," with a possible symptom score ranging from 0 to 36.

The distribution was as follows:

0	-- no symptoms	10%
1-5	-- very few symptoms	44%
6-10	-- occasional symptoms	38%
11+	-- frequent symptoms	8%

Social and Emotional Adjustment of the Children

We asked the parents whether their child had been subjected to any cruelty by classmates or playmates because of her or his racial background. A third (33%) said that their child had not met with any cruelty, and almost a fifth (18%) indicated that no such problem could arise because the child's peers did not know about her or his racial background. Almost half (49%) of the parents reported that their child had been subjected to some type of cruelty, usually name-calling or heckling, and, occasionally, physical abuse.

Despite the problems that so many of these children have encountered, the vast majority of them have several very close or fairly close friends. Although the parents perceive 8% of the children as not particularly popular or quite unpopular, only 2% are reported to have no close friends or playmates. More than half of the children with close friends have only

-34-

white friends, and 2% have only nonwhite friends. For 8% of the children their "best friends" are black.

All but 3% of the children are described as getting along very well (60%) or moderately well (37%) with other children. When the parents were asked specifically how their child got along with older and with younger children, the responses were similar.

The parents were asked about several negative traits that might present difficulties for their child in relating to peers. Three of these traits were reported as true for at least a fourth of the children--too sensitive (35%), too bossy (29%) and too aggressive (25%). Only a few children were considered to have problems in peer relationships because of being too serious (2%) or because of fear of other children (11%).

For a large majority, relations with siblings were also highly satisfactory. Over three-fourths (78%) were said to get along well all or most of the time. The relationship between the adopted child and siblings was generally described as very or moderately warm and affectionate. Only 4% of the adopted children were described as being distant, antagonistic or jealous of their siblings, and similar feelings on the part of siblings toward the adopted child were said to be true in 3% of the cases. (See Table 2-5)

Table 2-5

Relationship Between Adopted Child and Siblings

Feelings	Child Toward Siblings (N=116) %	Siblings Toward Child (N=114) %
Very warm and affectionate	44	46
Moderately warm and affectionate	47	43
Some warm, others antagonistic or distant	5	8
No affection, distant	2	2
Antagonistic, jealous	2	1
Total	100	100

Formal religion apparently plays a part in the lives of two-thirds of the children, most of these attending church, synagogue or Sunday School regularly. On the other hand, three-fourths of the children belong to some recreational or group-work organization such as the Scouts, the Y, an athletic team, etc., and a fifth of the children belong to and regularly attend three or more such groups.

The children tended to score higher on personal adjustment as compared with social adjustment on the California Test of Personality. On their total adjustment scores on this test these children compared favorably with white adopted children. In a followup study of white children who had been adopted by white families, Hoopes et al.[2] found that 22% of the children

2. Janet L. Hoopes, Edmund A. Sherman, Elizabeth A. Lawder, Roberta G. Andrews and Katherine D. Lower, A Followup Study of Adoptions (Vol.II): Post-Placement Functioning of Adopted Children. Child Welfare League of America, 1970, p.43.

scored at the 20th percentile or below, a score which they
rated as poor adjustment, and that 47% of the children scored
at the 50th percentile or above, a score which they described
as indicating an adequate or good adjustment. As can be seen
from Table 2-6, the distribution of the transracially adopted
(TRA) children was almost identical with the Hoopes findings,
with 21% at or below the 20th percentile and 47% at or above
the 50th percentile.

Table 2-6

Total Adjustment Scores on the California Test of
Personality of TRA Children and White
Inracial Adopted Children

Percentile Rank on Test	TRA Children (N=111) %	White Adopted Children (N=100) %
2nd	--)	1)
5th	1)	2)
10th	6) 21	5) 22
20th	14)	14)
30th	13	14
40th	19	17
50th	11)	9)
60th	13)	7)
70th	10)	11)
80th	7) 47	7) 47
90th	4)	10)
95th	2)	2)
98th	--)	1)
Total	100	100

How easy or difficult had the parents found the rearing of these children? At Time 1 well over two-fifths of both the mothers and the fathers reported that it had been easy, about a fourth said that it had been average, and less than a third felt that it had been difficult. At Time 2 the proportion of parents describing their child as hard to rear dropped somewhat. When asked to compare the ease or difficulty of rearing this child with that of their other children, about the same proportion of parents reported this child easier as reported this child harder to rear than their other children.

For those parents reporting that they found the child rearing easy, the reason most frequently given (80% of those cases) related to some positive aspect of the child's personality or disposition--e.g., the youngster has a good sense of humor, is even-tempered, thoughtful, etc. Similarly, but with far less frequency, the child's personality was given as the reason for difficulties. Over half the parents who reported that their child was difficult to rear attributed this to the child's being temperamental, short-tempered, stubborn, moody or the like, but about a fourth of the parents reported problems stemming from the fact that the child was older when entering their home and presented difficulties because of her or his earlier life experiences.

The Adoptive Parents

At the time of the child's placement in their home the majority of both the mothers (58%) and the fathers (56%) on whom we have these data were between the ages of 30 and 39. Five mothers and two fathers were under 25, and seven fathers were 50 years of age or older. The median age for the mothers was 34.0 years, and for the fathers, 36.7. At the time of the first interview, which occurred on the average about 7 years after the adoptive placement, the median ages were 42.2 and 44.1, respectively. (Table 2-7)

Table 2-7

Ages of Mothers and Fathers at Placement
and at Time 1 Interview

| | At Placement | | | | At Time 1 | | | |
| | Mother | | Father | | Mother | | Father | |
	No.	%	No.	%	No.	%	No.	%
Under 25	5	4	2	12	--	--	--	--
25 - 29	21	18	10	9	3	3	1	1
30 - 34	39	34	32	30	11	10	4	4
35 - 39	27	24	28	26	29	25	22	21
40 - 44	16	14	21	20	33	29	32	30
45 - 49	7	6	7	7	27	23	24	22
50 or more	--	--	7	7	12	10	24	22
Total	115	100	107	100*	115	100	107	100
Unknown	10		15		10		7	
Not applicable	--		3		--		11	
Median	34.0		36.7		42.2		44.1	

* Total does not add to 100 because of rounding.

Three single-parent adoptions--all by women--were included in the study population. At the time of placement the length of marriage of the 122 adoptive couples had ranged from less than 5 years (11%) to 20 years or more (5%). A third of the couples had been married between 5 and 9 years and another third between 10 and 14 years. At Time 1, 93% were still married, 4% were divorced and the remainder were widowed. Only one parent had remarried during the interim--about a year before the first interview. The relatively high marital stability was maintained between Time 1 and Time 2; during that period only one couple separated, and one divorced mother and one single mother married.

Household Composition

The household composition of the majority of these families (86%) was that of the typical nuclear family, consisting of mother, father and one or more children. In a few instances (6% of the families) other related or nonrelated adults shared the adoptive couple's home. In eight of the 11 homes in which there was only the adoptive mother present, the family consisted of mother and one or more children, and in three homes other adults were also present.

Most of the families were caring for one or more children--biological, adopted or foster--at the time the study child was placed. Seventy percent of the families had biological children at the time of the placement, and at Time 1 66%

had biological children still living at home. Between the time
of placement and the Time 1 interview, family size, excluding
the study child, increased slightly from a median of 2.30 children to 2.65. (Table 2-8)

Table 2-8

Number of Children (Exclusive of Study Child) in Home at Time
of Placement and at Time 1 Interview

Number of Children	At Placement		Time 1	
	No.	%	No.	%
0	18	14	9	7
1	22	18	16	13
2	28	22	32	25
3	30	24	36	29
4	11	9	16	13
5	12	10	9	7
6 or more	4	3	7	6
Total	125	100	125	100
Median	2.30		2.65	

At the time of placement about a third of the families
already had one or more adopted children. At Time 1, excluding
our study child, these 125 families had adopted or were adopting a total of 171 children. The median number of such children was 1.03. Slightly more than a third of the families
had no other adopted or pre-adoptive children in their home,
but over half had from one to three, and several had four or
more. (Table 2-9)

Table 2-9

Number of Other Adoptive and Pre-Adoptive
Children in Home at Any Time

Number	Other Adoptive Children	
	No.	%
0	45	36
1	33	26
2	22	18
3	15	12
4	4	3
5	5	4
8	1	1
Total	125	100
Median	1.03	

The study child was usually not the only child from a racial minority whom the family had adopted. Of those families who had other adopted or pre-adoptive children at Time 1, 57% had children of black or part-black parentage and 26% had children from other minority groups.

The Parents' Socioeconomic Status

Consistent with the findings of other studies, the adoptive parents tended to have a high educational level. Over two-thirds of the fathers were college graduates and almost half had advanced degrees. Similarly, about half of the mothers were college graduates, and an appreciable number had advanced degrees. Only 4% of all the mothers and fathers had not completed high school. (Table 2-10)

Table 2-10

Socioeconomic Characteristics of the Adoptive Parents

Education	Mother No.	Mother %	Father No.	Father %
Less than high school	5	4	5	4
High school graduate	27	22	16	14
Some college	33	26	16	14
College graduate	42	34	26	23
Post college degree	18	14	52	45
Total	125	100	115*	100

Employment	Mother No.	Mother %	Father No.	Father %
Professional, technical	35	28	64	56
Manager, proprietor	3	2	22	19
Clerical and sales	8	6	10	9
Skilled labor	1	1	7	6
Semiskilled labor	2	2	2	2
Homemaker	75	60	--	--
Not employed	--	--	5	4
Unknown	1	1	5	4
Total	125	100	115*	100

Annual Family Income	Mother No.	Mother %
Under $5,000	2	2
5,000 - 9,999	14	11
10,000 - 14,999	42	34
15,000 - 19,999	27	22
20,000 and above	39	31
Unknown	1	1
Total	125	100

* Includes new spouse of one adopting mother.

In view of their high educational attainment, it is not surprising that well over half the fathers were in professional or technical positions, and that another fifth were managers or proprietors. Two-fifths of the mothers were employed, with the majority of these in professional and technical categories.

At Time 1 the median annual family income was $15,700. More than a tenth of the families had incomes under $10,000, but almost a third had incomes of $20,000 or more. In a majority of the families, the adoptive father was the only one employed outside the home, but in 30% both wife and husband had outside employment and in 10% the adoptive mother was the sole wage earner. In three families neither parent had outside employment.

Community Characteristics

As indicated earlier, the children had been living with their adoptive parents for from 3 to 18 years. Given the mobility of American society, it was not surprising to find that only 58% of the families interviewed at Time 1 were still living in the neighborhood where they lived prior to the study child's entrance into their home. Of those who had changed neighborhoods, about a third had been in their current location more than 5 years, a third from 2 to 5 years, and the remaining third less than 2 years.

The regional distribution of the participating families at time of followup was as follows:

Pacific	28%
New England	23%
West North Central	20%
Canada	15%
East North Central	13%
Middle Atlantic	1%

As may be seen from Table 2-11, a majority of the families lived in communities of under 50,000 population and less than a tenth in communities with populations of 1 million or more. Two-thirds of the families lived in cities or towns with a nonwhite population of less than 5%, and only 17% lived in communities with a nonwhite population of 10% or more.

Table 2-11

Size and Racial Composition of Community
in Which Family Was Residing at Time 1

Population (1970 Census)	No.	%	Percent Nonwhite	No.
Under 10,000	24	19	Under 5%	67
10,000 - 24,999	26	21	5 - 9%	16
25,000 - 49,999	22	18	10 - 24%	10
50,000 - 99,999	18	15	25 - 49%	7
100,000 - 499,999	16	13		
500,000 - 999,999	7	6		
1,000,000 and above	10	8		
			Total	100
Total	123	100	Unknown	25
Unknown	2			

With few exceptions, the families described their immediate neighborhoods as totally white (45%) or predominantly white (45%). The 56 families who reported that their neighborhoods were all white were queried about the effect of this on their black study child. About a third felt that it did or could create difficulties, and a fifth said such a neighborhood presented mixed blessings. The reason usually given for potential problems was the child's lack of opportunity for exposure to other blacks. Other reasons given were the negative reaction of neighbors, the child's feeling of being different, and, on the other hand, the preferential treatment accorded the child by the neighbors because of this difference. About a tenth said that the racial composition of the neighborhood made no difference, and an almost equal proportion felt that their black child was better off living in an all-white neighborhood. The latter parents frequently reasoned that, because there were no other minority groups in the neighborhood, the neighbors had no pre-established prejudices toward blacks. Other reasons given were that the neighborhood was better for the family as a whole, it prepares the child for living in white society, or the neighborhood had better schools. In two instances the families said that living in an all-white neighborhood made it easier, since their child looked white and was accepted as white.

Between Time 1 and Time 2, eight families had moved for reasons unrelated to race, such as change in job, or the need for a larger house. Only one family moved to a more racially mixed neighborhood.

At Time 2, the 114 families were asked several questions concerning the social and political views of their neighbors. Of those responding, 53% believed their neighbors to be fairly conservative, 41% described their neighbors as fairly liberal, and the few remaining families usually said that their neighborhood was a mixture of liberals and conservatives. Sixty-one percent believed most of their neighbors voted for Nixon in the

1972 presidential election, 28% believed most voted for McGovern, 5% said their neighbors were evenly divided, and the remaining 6% just didn't know.* Asked their neighbors' opinions on busing of black children into the neighborhood,* 51% believed their neighbors would not approve, 37% thought they would, and 12% did not know. Neighbors were thought to be somewhat more liberal on accepting black families, or on more black families moving to their neighborhood, than they were believed to be on busing. Only 33% felt that their neighbors would not approve, whereas 58% believed that they would; the remaining 9% refused to guess how their neighbors might react.

Life Styles of the Parents

Close to 90% of the parents reported a religious affiliation and over 60% of these said that they attend religious services regularly. About two-thirds of the adoptive mothers and fathers--66% and 65% respectively--are Protestant. Catholics compose the next largest religious group--15% of the mothers and 16% of the fathers. Seven percent of the mothers and 8% of the fathers are Jewish. One set of parents holds membership in a church outside the three major denominations.

In the main, these appear to be rather self-contained families whose lives center pretty much on the nuclear family unit.

---

*These questions were asked only of United States residents.

Although slightly over half the parents reported having many friends or acquaintances, less than half exchange visits with friends more frequently than two or three times a month. Almost all (95%) of the families report engaging in leisure activities as a family unit. Sports were the single type of activity most frequently mentioned, but almost half the families listed a variety of activities that the family members enjoy together.

About two-thirds (66%) of the mothers and almost three-fifths (57%) of the fathers have relatives living in the area--usually parents and/or siblings. The majority of these parents maintain contact with relatives, with 67% of the mothers and 60% of the fathers seeing their relatives at least once a month. However, despite the physical proximity, almost a third (32%) of the mothers and half (50%) of the fathers report having no particularly close affectional ties to these relatives.

One might anticipate that white families who adopted children of black parentage, particularly during the period when such adoptions were uncommon and when the families may have been looked upon as being eccentric, would be socially and politically more progressive than the average family. At least on one dimension this certainly appears to be the case. When asked to describe at what point on a scale they would place themselves relative to their political and social views, 72% of the mothers and 62% of the fathers described themselves as liberal or extremely liberal, as compared with 58% of mothers and 54% of

fathers who adopted Indian children.[3] Only a tenth of the
mothers and 12% of the fathers in our sample placed themselves
in the conservative or extremely conservative categories, and
the remainder saw themselves as being "middle of the road."
This is in striking contrast to a survey of 1972 college fresh-
men conducted by the American Council on Education in which only
35% reported themselves as liberal.[4]

The Time 2 interviews took place after the 1972 elections.
During these interviews the parents were asked about their usual
party preferences, as well as how they had voted in the 1972
presidential election.[5] Slightly over half the mothers and
fathers--56% and 51%, respectively-- described themselves as
Democrats. About a fourth of the mothers (24%) and a third of
the fathers (32%) said they were Republicans. Another 2% of the
parents said they usually voted for a third party and the remainder described themselves as generally voting split tickets.

In his study of families who had adopted Indian children
Fanshel found that the voting patterns of the mothers in the 1956
and 1960 elections and of the fathers in 1956 were similar to
the national vote, though in the 1960 election the fathers

---

3. David Fanshel, Far From the Reservation. Metuchen, N.J.:
   Scarecrow Press, 1972, pp. 141-143; 195-196.

4. Behavior Today: The Weekly Newsletter, February 19, 1973,
   Vol. 4, No.8.

5. The 17 Canadian families were not, of course, included.

deviated from the national voting pattern, with 63% voting for Kennedy as compared with his nationwide vote of 50%.[6] The voting patterns of our study group differed markedly from the national vote in 1972. Whereas Nixon received 61% of the popular vote, only 27% of the families in which both parents voted similarly or in which only one parent voted, voted for him. In 64% of the families either both parents or the one parent who voted said they had voted for McGovern, and in 9% of the families one parent voted for Nixon and the other for McGovern. In instances in which the parents' votes differed, twice the proportion of mothers as of fathers voted for McGovern. This is consistent with the fact that proportionately more of the mothers than fathers had described themselves as liberal in their political and social views.

Child-Rearing Roles and Attitudes

Who makes the decisions in these families regarding the various types of activities permitted their child and the types of punishments administered? Do these parents appear to be strict or lenient as to the behavior they expect from their child? Each parent was asked who usually made decisions about activities the child was permitted to engage in, such as attending the movies, viewing television, visiting friends, and, in

---

6. Fanshel, Far From the Reservation, pp. 141-143; 195-196.

the case of older children, going out at night. The parents
were also asked whether decisions about bedtime and the type of
punishment administered were usually made by one parent or both.
The frequency distributions of the mothers' and fathers' responses were similar. In over half the families both parents
responded that some of the decisions are made by the mother,
while others are made by both parents together. About a fourth
of the fathers (26%) and a fifth of the mothers (18%) reported
that, on the items related to child care, the decisions are made
jointly. In no instance was the father reported to make all the
decisions, and only a small proportion of the parents reported
that the mothers always made all decisions about the child.

To explore parental expectations regarding their child's
behavior, each parent was asked to respond to a list of nine
items, indicating whether in each instance she or he considered
the item very important, somewhat important, not at all important, or contrary to her or his expectations. The list included
such items as the importance of children's immediately obeying
when told to do something; whether children should defend their
rights by fighting back; whether they should be free to express
disagreement with parents or other adults, and the like. To
develop an index of parental permissiveness, eight of these
items were each scored from 1 to 4, with the lowest score indicating the greatest expectation of conformity and parental or
adult control. Although the possible range of scores was 8 to

32, the actual scores ranged only from 10 to 28, with a con-
centration at 17-18. The median scores for the mothers and
fathers were similar--17.3 and 17.5, respectively. Those scor-
ing 16 or below were categorized as strict or expecting considerable conformity from their child; those who scored 17 or 18, as
moderate in their expectations; and those with scores of 19 or
more, as permissive. As can be seen from Table 2-12, a slightly
higher proportion of the fathers than of the mothers fall into
the strict category and into the permissive category, while more
of the mothers had moderate ratings.

Table 2-12
Parental Expectations Regarding Child's Conformity

	Mothers (N=124) %	Fathers (N=114) %
Strict (under 17)	32	36
Moderate (17-18)	38	28
Permissive (19 and above)	30	36
Total	100	100

Rearing a Black Child in a White Home

When asked about their contact with blacks prior to this
adoption, few of the families (7%) reported not being acquaint-
ed with any blacks, and over half the families (53%) reported
having black friends. About a third (32%) of the families said
that this adoption had resulted in their developing black friends
or increasing their contact with blacks. This is borne out by
the fact that at Time 1 four-fifths of the families reported

having black friends or acquaintances and three-fifths of all the adoptive families socialized with black friends or acquaintances in each others' homes.

Those opposed to transracial adoption have frequently voiced their concern about the child's loss of racial identity. At Time 1 we found that, although only 2% of the parents said that their child did not know that she or he was adopted, 14% of the parents reported that their child was, to their knowledge, unaware of her or his parents' racial background. At Time 2, eight of the 114 families seen (7%) still had not told their children about their parentage. Two of these families indicated they did not intend ever to reveal this information, justifying this decision on the basis not only that their child was Caucasian in appearance, but that the child's black ancestry was a fourth or less. Four other parents had not yet decided whether they would share this information, and the other two said they planned to tell their child in due time.

How important do the parents think it is for a child to know about her or his racial background? Do they find it easy or difficult to talk about this with their child? Do mothers and fathers have differing or similar opinions and attitudes on these questions of their child's parentage? How frequently do these parents discuss this matter with their children?

Despite the fact that 14% of the parents indicated that their child did not know of her or his place parentage, only 7%

of the mothers and 6% of the fathers ascribed little or no importance to a child's knowing about her or his racial background. More of the mothers (71%) than of the fathers (59%) expressed the opinion that it was very important for a child to have this information. Consistent with this is the finding that a far larger proportion of fathers than mothers--23% versus 12%--said they had never discussed racial background with their child. However, more of the mothers (13%) than of the fathers (5%) who have engaged their children in discussion of racial background admitted to finding discussion of this topic difficult. If parents do discuss racial background with their child, usually the discussion is on a fairly regular, ongoing basis.

At Time 2 we also asked the interviewer to rate the parents on a five-point scale regarding their acknowledgment of their child's being black, the degree that they felt the issue of the child's racial background created problems for the child and for the parents, and the degree of comfort the parents exhibited in the discussion of race-related questions. About equal percentages of the mothers and fathers--78% and 82%, respectively--were rated as accepting, that is, to have few or no problems in acknowledging the racial background of their child. Six percent of the parents were rated as midway between acceptance and denial, and 16% of the mothers and 12% of the fathers were rated as giving evidence of major or minor denial of their child's black background.

Over three-fourths of the parents (77%) were judged to be comfortable when discussing race-related questions, but more than a tenth (12%) were rated as somewhat or very uncomfortable. Similarly, for approximately three-fourths, the interviewers saw only minimal problems for the child (73%) and the parents (76%) because of their racial differences. Not surprisingly, ratings of somewhat severe or very severe problems were seen somewhat more frequently for the child than for the parents--9% versus 5%.

Racial Orientation of the Adoptive Parents

Other than their contact with black friends, how well related are these families to the "black scene"? How aware and concerned are they about problems their child might encounter because of being black? Do they attempt to provide their child and themselves with exposure to the black media, etc.? To enhance their awareness and sensitivity, do they have contact with others who have adopted transracially? As a result of what their friends have observed, do any of these friends ever talk with them about the possibility of adopting transracially?

Depending upon how one wishes to "read" their responses, a rather dismaying or a rather heartening third of the parents said that they did not anticipate that their child would encounter any difficulties due to her or his racial background. Of those who anticipated problems, 15% expressed serious concern and 30% moderate concern, but 37% said they were only slightly concerned, and a rather amazing 18% reported no concern at all, apparently feeling that the child had sufficient inner strength and security to withstand any difficulties encountered.

When asked about specific things they had done to further their own awareness or to expose their child to black history or culture, the vast majority of families (85%) reported having read, or having in their homes, books written by or about blacks. Usually those books focused on current racism, although some families reported having biographies and children's books in their homes. However, of the families who had utilized this method of self-advancement or development of racial awareness and pride in their child, only 44% had found such reading helpful.

Other methods utilized by some of the parents have been trips to museums or special black cultural events, activities reported by 29% of the families. About one of every 10 families subscribed to black newspapers, and almost a third reported having black magazines such as Ebony or Jet in their homes.

At Time 1, nearly two-thirds (64%) of the families were maintaining contact with others who had adopted transracially, usually as members of a transracial adoptive parent group but in about a third of the cases through informal association with other families who like themselves had adopted children of a different race. Approximately two-thirds of the parents--68% of the mothers and 66% of the fathers--had been approached by friends interested in discussing transracial adoption. Indeed, 36% of the mothers and 41% of the fathers reported that following such discussion their friends had adopted or were in the process of adopting a child of another race.

When each parent, regardless of whether she or he had been approached on this subject by a friend or acquaintance, was asked what advice she or he would give, a fourth of the mothers and about a third of the fathers indicated they would strongly encourage the inquiring person to adopt transracially. About one in seven of both the mothers and the fathers replied they would not take on the role of advice-giver. With the exception of three parents who did not know how they would respond and one who would mildly discourage such a step, the parents believed they would encourage their friends but with certain qualifications, such as cautioning them about potential difficulties and/ or encouraging only those friends who they thought were well equipped to adopt transracially. Most frequently mentioned as persons who they felt should not undertake such adoptions were individuals who might be adopting out of guilt or a sense of duty. Many thought families who lived in communities in which there was considerable racial prejudice, and parents whose extended families disapproved of such adoptions, would be unsuccessful transracial adoptive parents. Persons who are "status-conscious" or "establishment-oriented" were mentioned by a lesser number of parents as not suited to adopt transracially. A small number of respondents mentioned persons who were themselves prejudiced and persons whose immaturity or instability would make them poor adoptive parents in any case.

Parental Attitudes Toward Blacks

It has been the contention of some that many persons who adopt transracially may, in fact, be racially prejudiced themselves. An exploration of the literature and of the various tests dealing with prejudice and discrimination revealed no standardized instruments that seemed appropriate to test this issue with adoptive parents. After consultation with persons sensitive to subtle racist attitudes, we therefore developed a set of statements that might indicate racist or nonracist attitudes. These were pretested on black and white volunteers whose general attitudes on race were known to the project director. The set of statements was then modified and was included in the individual parent questionnaire. The parents were asked to check the degree of their agreement or disagreement with each statement on a Likert-type scale. Although in general the instrument has face validity, its reliability is untested.

A considerable majority of both fathers and mothers agreed with three of these statements directed to attitudes about the development of black pride or racial awareness in their children. As can be seen from Table 2-13, from 75% to 93% of the mothers were in agreement, although fairly substantial proportions were uncertain as to the importance of acquainting their children with the contributions of some of the black leaders and of helping their black children identify with the black community. The agreement of the fathers with each of these statements was somewhat lower than that of the mothers. In fact, a fifth of the fathers disagreed with the importance of their children's becoming familiarized with the contribution of black leaders, and almost a fifth expressed uncertainty about the importance of helping their children acquire a feeling of identity with the black community.

A second set of statements was directed to other aspects of rearing a black child. As may be seen from Table 2-14, roughly half of the mothers and of the fathers agreed with each of the four statements, but there were slight differences between the parents. More of the mothers agreed with the statements that 1) the tasks of parents rearing a black child are no different from those of parents rearing a white child, and 2) love and security are sufficient to prepare a black child for adulthood. Slightly fewer mothers than fathers agreed that a black child is likely to have identity problems. On the other hand, slightly more mothers agreed to the importance of having or acquiring black friends.

Table 2-13

Parental Response to Development of Black Pride

Statements	Mothers (N=109-112)			Fathers (N=104-105)		
	Agree %	Un-certain %	Dis-agree %	Agree %	Un-certain %	Dis-agree %
It's very important for a black or part-black child to develop pride in her or his black heritage.	93	2	5	86	4	10
Parents should make their black or part-black child aware of contributions of such black leaders as Stokely Carmichael, Malcolm X and Eldridge Cleaver.	81	13	6	72	8	20
Black children adopted by white families should be helped to acquire a feeling of identity with the black community.	75	16	9	66	18	6

Table 2-14

Parental Role in Rearing a Black Child

Statements	Mothers (N=107-110)			Fathers (N=102-105)		
	Agree %	Un-certain %	Dis-agree %	Agree %	Un-certain %	Dis-agree %
The tasks that parents have in rearing a black child are no different from those of parents rearing a white child.	50	5	45	42	9	49
It is essential that white families who adopt trans-racially have or acquire black friends.	49	15	36	43	10	47
A black child reared by white parents is likely to have problems in developing a sense of identity.	44	15	41	49	17	34
A black child is sufficiently prepared for adulthood if given love and security by her or his white adoptive parents.	54	11	35	48	21	31

A third set of statements consisting of 14 items was mainly concerned with the political-social consciousness of the adoptive parents. Three indices were developed from the items with significant intercorrelations: a 10-item index of the mothers' attitudes toward blacks, an 11-item index of the fathers' attitudes, and a 4-item index to describe the joint parental attitudes.

The responses indicate that the majority of these parents exhibit a high degree of political-social consciousness with regard to blacks and other minority groups. On 12 of the 14 statements over two-thirds of the mothers took a liberal or politically conscious stance, and on nine of the statements this was true of the fathers. The only statement that provoked a substantial number of uncertain responses, and this on the part of the mothers, concerned the government's role in equalizing opportunities for minority groups. The one statement that did run counter to what had been anticipated to be the response of white parents who have adopted black children was the statement directed to whether they saw racism as affecting their lives very much. Over half of the mothers and fathers disagreed with this statement, apparently feeling that their lives have not been particularly affected by racism.

Table 2-15

Parents' Political-Social Attitudes

Statements	Mothers (N=108-112)			Fathers (N=102-105)		
	Agree %	Un-certain %	Dis-agree %	Agree %	Un-certain %	Dis-agree %
Our government isn't doing as much as it can to provide opportunities for minority groups. (a,d)	69	18	13	73	11	16
Many of the black groups today are pushing for too much change too quickly. (a,d)	13	10	77	26	12	62
Today's blacks should take heart from our immigrant groups who got ahead by working hard and by saving. (b)	14	10	76	20	20	60
Most of the complaints today about racial inequality are not justified by the facts. (a,d)	12	13	75	13	9	78
Blacks are not to blame for the fact that so many of them are poor. (c)	86	7	7	81	7	12
A poor white youth will have as much trouble getting ahead as will a poor black youth. (b)	19	11	70	15	7	78
There is far too much emphasis today on racial equality. (c)	11	10	79	18	7	75
Most of today's black leaders are "pushy" and overdemanding. (a)	6	15	79	12	13	75
America has always been a land of opportunity for those who really want to get ahead. (a)	28	5	67	37	10	53
The reason so many blacks are on welfare is because they do not know how to manage their lives properly. (b)	7	10	83	10	7	83
White students should take courses in black history and black culture. (c)	92	4	4	77	12	11

Table 2-15 (continued)

Parents' Political-Social Attitudes

Statements	Mothers (N=108-112)			Fathers (N=102-105)		
	Agree %	Un-certain %	Dis-agree %	Agree %	Un-certain %	Dis-agree %
Our administration is doing a great deal to equalize opportunities for all races. (a,d)	18	26	56	25	15	60
Racism does not affect my life very much. (c)	44	4	52	45	3	52
Blacks and other minority groups expect too great a change in too short a time. (a)	9	9	82	22	6	72

a = Statements used in both mothers' and fathers' indices
b = Statements used in mothers' index only
c = Statements used in fathers' index only
d = Statements used in joint parental index

Summary

The study children varied widely in age and length of time
in the adoptive home, with the typical child having spent most
of her 9 years with her adoptive parents. Most of the children
were reported by both teachers and parents as doing well in
school. Their physical health tended to be good and they were
relatively free of somatic symptoms. An overwhelming majority
had good relations with siblings and with other children, and
showed little indication of emotional difficulty.

Few of the children were the only child in the home at
time of placement. Most were adopted by two-parent families
of high educational level. At followup the father was usually
employed in a professional or technical position, and in a
substantial proportion of cases the mother was similarly employed. The families tended to live in totally or predominantly white neighborhoods in relatively small communities.
Most were liberal in political-social orientation, more so than
their neighbors.

The parents were likely to share in decisions about the
child. One characteristic on which they were least homogeneous
was in their permissiveness toward the child, with strict and
permissive attitudes equally common.

A majority of the families have black friends and visit
back and forth in each others' homes, and most of the parents

have told their children about their racial background. According-
ing to the interviewers, acknowledgment of the child's racial
background was not a problem for the majority of these parents.
However, at one time or another about half the children are
known to have been subjected to teasing or other types of cruelty by their peers because of their racial background.

Chapter 3

THE ADOPTION EXPERIENCE

Considerable attention was given in the parent interviews
and questionnaires to the parents' adoption experience. The
areas explored ranged from their initial motivation for adoption to the satisfactions and dissatisfactions in adopting the
study child.

Motivation for Adoption

We asked the parents to think back to the period prior to
their adopting the study child and to tell us why they had considered adopting in the first place. The reason most commonly
given was infertility or fear of another pregnancy, but almost
as many families seemed to have considered adoption out of
societal concern, particularly concern about children's not
having homes. A few wanted larger families, but did not want
to contribute to an increase in the world population. A few
others had not thought about adopting until approached by a
social agency. A small number said they had thought about
adopting because of their love for children and their ability
to provide both physically and emotionally for them. Only
three families indicated they had been prompted solely by their
interest in furthering the cause of integration by adopting a
child of another race.

A third of the families attributed their thinking about adoption to what we have labeled circumstantial or personal reasons. Almost half of this group had foster children to whom they became attached and whom they subsequently adopted. A sizable group saw adoption as a means of obtaining a child of a specific sex and/or age, usually to fit into their family scheme. Some families thought of adoption as a means of providing companionship for their own child. In some instances the idea of adopting occurred after the families saw a child in whom they became particularly interested. (Table 3-1)

Table 3-1

Reasons Given by Parents for Considering
the Possibility of Adoption

Reasons	No.	%
Infertility or fear of pregnancy	48	38
Social motivation	43	34
Concern for children without homes	25	20
Population explosion prohibits having more biological children	6	5
Social agency approached them	5	4
"Room for one more"	4	3
Facilitate integration	3	2
Circumstantial, personal and other	34	28
Became attached to foster child	16	13
To get a child of certain specification	8	6
Companionship for own child	5	4
Wanted a child they happened to see	2	2
Unclear	3	3
Total	125	100

When asked whether they had had a preference with regard to the racial background of the child, almost three-fifths expressed no preference. On the other hand, about a fifth of the families were specifically interested in adopting a black child, and an equal proportion were interested in adopting a child of some other minority group. Only one family indicated that, when they first considered adoption, they had a white child in mind.

Motivation for Adopting a Black Child

In a later series of questions during the Time 1 interview, inquiry was made into such areas as the parents' reasons for deciding to adopt a black child and the concern they had in adopting transracially. For 29% of the families the idea of adopting transracially was first suggested by someone else, usually an agency social worker. Only 12% of the families said they had known someone who had adopted a child of another race. For 61% the decision to adopt was reached simultaneously by both parents, for 28% the adoptive mother first had the idea, and for 11% it was the father who first thought of transracial adoption.

Of several reasons advanced for deciding to adopt transracially, the most common one we labeled "social motivation." Typically, these persons were concerned about black children who seemed doomed to long-time foster care. For good or ill, there were a few in this category who viewed transracial adoption as a means of furthering the cause of

integration or as a way of carrying out their "Christian duty."
The reason given by two other families was that the assimilation
of a black child into their home would benefit the family as a
whole. (Table 3-2)

Table 3-2

Reason for Adopting Transracially

Reason	No.	%
Social motivation	68	54
Provide a home for hard-to-place child	53	42
Aid to integration; Christian duty	13	10
Integration a benefit to family	2	2
Personal motivation	40	32
Wanted a child, race unimportant	28	22
Became attached to foster child	10	8
Knew child; made parents feel special	2	2
Second choice	14	12
No other children available	12	10
Assurance that child looks Caucasian	2	2
Unclear	3	2
Total	125	100

About a third of the families specified reasons that seemed
to be more directly concerned with their individual needs or
their personal experiences. The majority of these families
"just wanted a child." Others decided to adopt transracially
after their experience of having the child in their home on a
foster care basis. In one instance the decision came about

after knowing the child in the community, and in another case
the parents saw transracial adoption as a means of making them
feel different or "special."

For more than one of every 10 families (12%) the decision
to adopt transracially appeared to have been made after learning that these were the only children they would be able to
adopt. Most of these families acknowledged that transracial
adoption was not their original choice. In the case of two
families, they indicated that they had decided upon this course
of action only after assurance that the child would not be dis-
similar to them in appearance.

Reservations About Transracial Adoption

We asked the parents whether, at the time they first began
to consider adopting transracially, they had any reservations
about it. A variety of possible concerns were listed and the
parents were asked to tell us whether in each instance they
were considerably worried, somewhat worried, or not at all
worried.

As can be seen in Table 3-3, the item that caused the
greatest concern was how the parents' extended families would
react to their adopting transracially. Forty-five percent of
the mothers and 47% of the fathers said they had been concerned about this. The two other items of greatest concern--
true for about two-fifths of both the mothers and the fathers--
were more directly related to the child's immediate environ-

-71-

ment and sense of belonging--how the child would be treated by children in the neighborhood and whether she or he would be happy having white parents. Less than a fourth of the parents reported having been concerned about each of the other potential problems, and with few exceptions the concern was moderate. In the few instances in which there were differences of opinion between the parents, the fathers tended to have slightly greater misgivings.

Table 3-3

Reservations About Adopting Transracially

(Mothers: N=125; Fathers: N=114)

Area of Concern	Degree of Concern					
	Considerable		Moderate		None	
	Mo. %	Fa. %	Mo. %	Fa. %	Mo. %	Fa. %
Feeling like a parent to an adopted child	2	2	12	14	86	84
Feeling like a parent to a child of a different race	1	3	10	13	89	84
Extended family's reaction to adoption	6	6	17	18	77	76
Extended family's reaction to transracial adoption	10	10	35	37	55	53
How black child would fit into family	--	--	23	23	77	77
What neighbors might think	1	1	16	17	83	82
How neighborhood children would treat black child	3	3	36	37	61	60
Whether black child would be happy with white parents	7	7	33	33	60	60

In view of the parents' concern about the anticipated
reactions of relatives, it is appropriate to discuss the actual
reactions reported by the adoptive parents. Slightly more than
half of the mothers and fathers (57% and 55%) said that from
the beginning all of their relatives were supportive. Although
a third of the parents said that all of their relatives had dis-
liked the idea in the beginning, in the majority of these cases
the relatives eventually came around to accepting it. Not surprisingly, some parents reported reactions that varied from
relative to relative. Of major interest is the fact that some
or all of the relatives are still opposed to the adoption in
the case of 9% of the mothers and 12% of the fathers. In addition, another 5% of the mothers and 3% of the fathers have never
told their relatives of their adopted child's black heritage.
The parents in most instances attributed the opposition of relatives not to the idea of adoption, but specifically to the child's
racial background.

Openness to Adoption of Atypical Adoptive Children

Using the format developed by Fanshel for his study of
families who adopted Indian children,[1] the parents were queried
about their willingness to adopt children of various racial or
ethnic backgrounds, older children, and children with actual or

---

1. David Fanshel, Far From the Reservation. Metuchen, N.J.:
   Scarecrow Press, 1972.

potential handicaps. The question asked was whether the parent
felt that, if offered a child with the particular characteristic,
she or he could have adopted this child easily, with minor reservations, with major reservations, or would not have considered
the child at all.

The child's racial or ethnic background seemed to matter
little to these parents. With few exceptions the mothers and
the fathers said that they would have easily adopted an American
Indian, Mexican-American, Oriental or Puerto Rican child.

In the Fanshel study of white couples who had adopted
American Indian children, the only racial groups the parents
were asked about were Oriental children and those of mixed black-
white parentage. A little more than two-thirds of the mothers
and fathers in that study would have easily adopted an Oriental
child, a significantly smaller proportion than in the current
study. Only about a fifth of the couples who adopted Indian
children could have adopted with ease a child of mixed black-
white parentage who was not obviously black in appearance, and
an even smaller proportion would have had no reservations about
a child who was obviously black.

However, the parents in our study indicated considerably
less openness to the possibility of adoption of older or handicapped children than of children of different ethnic background.
Table 3-4 gives comparative data from the current study and the
Fanshel study on the proportion of parents who would have easily

adopted older or handicapped children. A slightly higher percentage of mothers adopting Indian children than of mothers adopting black children were open to adopting a child with a serious correctable handicap. Although few of either study group were open to a child with a serious noncorrectable handicap, proportionately more of the parents in Fanshel's study expressed readiness to adopt such a child.

Table 3-4

Parents' Openness Toward Adoption of Handicapped and Older
Children

Percentage Adopting Easily

	Current Study		Indian Adoption Study	
	Mother (N=124-125) %	Father (N=113-114) %	Mother (N=92-97) %	Father (N=88-94) %
Child with serious correctable handicap (e.g., club foot)	39	31	45	31
Child with serious noncorrectable handicap (e.g., deaf, blind)	6	6	13	12
Normal child, 8 years or older	23*	32	40	35
Child with mental illness in immediate background	20*	14*	38	36
Slightly retarded child	8	5*	9	14

---

* Significant difference between parents adopting black and
Indian children.

Relatively few of the families (9%) had been particularly
interested in an infant under 3 months of age, 28% preferred a
child between 3 months and 3 years old, and 18% preferred a
child at least 3 years old, but 43% had no age preference. Only
a minority were, however, open to a normal child 8 years of age
or older; 23% of our mothers and 32% of our fathers would have
readily considered such a child, smaller proportions than applied to parents adopting Indian children. Only a fifth of our
mothers and a seventh of our fathers would have adopted easily
a child with mental illness in his immediate background, compared
with over a third of the parents adopting Indian children. Again,
although few parents in either group were open to adopting a
slightly retarded child, a significantly larger proportion of
fathers adopting Indian children than of those adopting black
children were open to this type of handicap.

In summary then, whereas the families who had adopted black
children indicated more acceptance of the possibility of adopting
children from other racial minority groups, one or both parents
in families who had adopted Indian children tended to indicate
more willingness to consider adopting children with various non-
racial handicapping characteristics. It would appear that these
parents represent two distinct groups of potential adoptive families for waiting children.

Attitude Toward the Adoption Agency

The interviewers explored with the parents the extent to
which their preferences had been discussed with the adoption
agency social worker and the adequacy of the information the
worker provided about the child and his background. From these
specific questions and the parents' general comments, the interviewers assessed the families' general satisfaction with their
agency contacts.

Excluding families whose decision to adopt came about following the placement of the child in their home as a foster child
and those who were approached by an agency about taking a specific
child, it was found that the social workers had explored with
over 90% of the parents their preference for a girl or a boy.
About two-thirds (66%) of the parents reported that the social
worker had inquired whether they had any preference regarding the
child's complexion or skin coloring, and slightly over a fifth
(22%) had been asked whether they preferred a child of black or
mixed parentage. Nearly two-thirds (63%) said that the social
worker had inquired about their preference with respect to the
prospective child's intellectual potential.   •

Although no preference regarding the race of the child's
parents and the child's skin coloring was expressed by well over
three-fifths of the adoptive applicants (69% and 61%, respectively),
about three-fourths (72%) of the parents had a preference regarding the sex of the child, and the vast majority (86%) who

had a preference reported that they had received a child of the sex preferred. Two-thirds of the parents had expressed a preference regarding the child's intellectual potential, and these were equally divided between parents preferring a child of high intellectual potential and those preferring a child of average intelligence. Well over half (56%) of these parents reported that their child met their intellectual specifications, a fourth (25%) of the parents believed the intellectual potential of their child to be superior to their original preference, and the remainder (19%) reported that their adopted child had a lower intellectual potential than they had originally desired.

Were these parents satisfied with the agency contact? In retrospect, did the parents feel that the social worker had given sufficient information about the child they were adopting? What attitude did they convey to the interviewer about their agency contact?

About four-fifths (81%) of the parents reported that they had received sufficient data about their adopted child's natural parents. On the other hand, only three-fourths (76%) found sufficient the information given them about the child's personality and about the child's habits, and only two-thirds (67%) felt that the social worker had informed them adequately about their adoptive child's experience prior to this placement. The information most frequently lacking concerned the child's medical problems, physical handicap or detailed medical history. Four families said they should have been told more about their child's emotional problems, and six reported that they had wanted additional information about the adopted child's racial background.

The reason most often given for having wanted further information was that it would have helped the parents cope with the child, facilitated the early adjustment, or enabled them to handle problems at an earlier stage. In four instances the parents said that additional information would have relieved their anxiety, and two families reported that, had they been aware of the facts about the child, they would not have chosen to adopt this particular child.

The interviewers felt that the general attitudes of three-fourths of the mothers and of the fathers toward the adoptive agency was positive. Over a tenth of the mothers and the fathers--11% and 13%, respectively--were described as having negative attitudes, and the rest were rated as neutral.

Satisfactions With the Adopted Child

How satisfied are these parents with the child? Have things turned out as well as expected? Did this adoption have any effect on the parents' relationship with each other? Are there any special satisfactions or dissatisfactions concerned with the adoption? How long did it take these parents before they felt the child was their own? Are there times when the parents have been especially glad about adopting this child or when they have regretted it? Do they have strong convictions about transracial adoption?

These were the questions explored to assess parental satisfaction. Approximately seven of every 10 mothers (69%) said that their experience with the study child had been extremely satisfying. About a fourth (23%) reported that they were more satisfied than dissatisfied, and another 5% described their feelings as varying between being satisfied and dissatisfied. Only 3% of the mothers indicated that they had found their experience to be more unsatisfactory than satisfactory (1%) or extremely unsatisfactory (2%).

The response of the fathers was even more positive, with over three-fourths (77%) describing this experience as extremely satisfying and another 17% saying it was more satisfying than dissatisfying. Four percent of the fathers indicated that there was an equal mix of satisfaction and dissatisfaction, and the remaining 2% described their experience as being more unsatisfactory than satisfactory.

Asked how they felt "things had turned out" insofar as the adoption was concerned, again the response of the fathers was somewhat more positive. Slightly more than two-fifths (41%) of the fathers, as compared with a third of the mothers (33%), reported that the adoption had turned out better than anticipated. Seven percent of the mothers but only 2% of the fathers felt it had turned out worse. The remainder--60% of the mothers and 57%

of the fathers--indicated that things had turned out pretty much as expected.

Changes in the family through birth, death or other circumstances not only affect the family as a unit, but also frequently have an impact on the relationships between the husband and wife. If the responses of the parents in this study are a true reflection of the facts, the adoption of these children was no exception. We asked the parents whether they felt that the addition of the child to their family had made their marriage happier or less happy. A third (33%) of the mothers and a fourth (25%) of the fathers said there had been no change in their marital relationship. On the other hand, 63% of the mothers and 70% of the fathers reported that their marriages were somewhat or much happier. Only 4% of the mothers and 5% of the fathers saw the adoption as being detrimental to their marriage.

A further substantiation of the parents' belief that the adopted child had made a difference in their relationship with each other, and also of the fathers' being more profoundly affected than the mothers, can be seen in Table 3-5. Each parent was given a list of items--12 possible benefits they might have felt they derived from having the child in their home--and was asked to indicate whether each benefit applied to them very much, much, a little, or not at all. Less than a fourth (23%) of the mothers and only 16% of the fathers said "not at all" to the statement, "Has made my marriage richer." On the other hand,

44% of the mothers and 54% of the fathers felt that the child had enriched their marriage to a considerable degree. About a fifth (19%) of the mothers and over one-third (36%) of the fathers felt that the child had had much or very much of an impact, bringing wife and husband closer together.

The benefit most frequently seen by the parents was the companionship given by the child, with 79% of the mothers and 75% of the fathers so reporting. The child's having enabled the parent to express her or his love was also reported by 71% of the mothers and 66% of the fathers. Perhaps because a large majority (86%) of these families had other children before this adoption occurred, the statement that the adoption experience had enabled the parent to fulfill her or his duty to have a family elicited the smallest proportions of positive responses--16% of the mothers and 19% of the fathers.

The only other item in which there was a notable difference between the responses of the mothers and fathers was the statement, "Has enabled me to give a home to a child whom nobody seemed to want." Whereas only about half (49%) of the mothers responded "very much" or "much" to the statement, this was true for three-fifths (60%) of the fathers.

Table 3-5

Effects of Adoption Experience on Parents

(Mothers: N=118-121)   (Fathers: N=110-113)

Possible Benefits	Very Much, Much Mother %	Very Much, Much Father %	A Little Mother %	A Little Father %	Not at All Mother %	Not at All Father %
Has enabled me to give a home to a child whom nobody seemed to want.	49	60	26	20	25	20
Has enabled me to fulfill my duty to have a family.	16	19	10	15	74	66
Has made me feel less lonely.	24	20	19	19	57	61
Has made me feel that I'm doing something toward furthering the cause of an integrated society.	31	38	44	41	25	21
Has enabled me to express the deep love for children I have always had.	71	66	22	19	7	15
Has brought my spouse and me closer together.	19	36	37	32	44	32
Has made me feel more like a "whole" person.	34	38	28	30	38	32
Has prevented me from becoming too selfish, too self-centered.	27	27	38	41	35	32
Has made me feel that I am helping to compensate for the inequities in our society.	23	22	37	46	40	32
Has made my marriage richer.	44	54	33	30	23	16
Has made me feel proud about being able to make a contribution to the community.	22	24	35	36	43	40
Has given me a great deal of satisfying companionship.	79	75	13	15	8	10

Each parent was asked to tell us what she or he found most satisfying and most dissatisfying about having the adopted child in their family. A few parents--4% of the mothers and 3% of the fathers--said they could think of no particularly satisfying things. On the other hand, about a fifth of the mothers (21%) and twice that proportion (42%) of the fathers could think of nothing dissatisfying. From half to two-thirds of those who specified most satisfying or dissatisfying aspects indicated that the satisfaction or dissatisfaction was derived from the child as a person. Attributes mentioned were the child's personality, disposition, physical appearance, emotional or physical health, and behavior. The role of parent was cited positively--the pleasure in parenting--by about one in six of the mothers, and negatively--the feeling of being tied down or the added responsibilities--by about the same number. It was cited positively by one in five of the fathers, and negatively by about one in seven. Another item frequently mentioned, usually positively, was the effect the child had on others. Seventeen percent of the mothers and 15% of the fathers reported this as the most satisfying thing, and 5% of the mothers and 8% of the fathers reported it as the most dissatisfying. (Table 3-6)

Table 3-6

Most Satisfying and Dissatisfying Things in
Having Child in Family

	Most Satisfying		Most Dissatisfying	
	Mother (N=114)* %	Father (N=104)* %	Mother (N=94)* %	Father (N=93)* %
Child as a person	55	50	65	61
Parental role	17	22	16	14
Effect of child's presence on others	17	15	5	8
Parent-child relationship	9	9	12	17
Other	2	4	2	--
Total	100	100	100	100

* Excludes respondents reporting none as well as those where the response was unclear.

Almost a tenth of the mothers and the fathers said that the parent-child relationship gave the most satisfaction. They commented on the affectional responses between parent and child or the feeling of mutuality or sharing. A somewhat larger proportion (12% of the mothers and 17% of the fathers) cited the parent-child relationship as the most dissatisfying thing, alluding to a lack of communication or affectional responses, or to their feeling of inadequacy at meeting the child's specific needs. An additional 2% of the mothers and 4% of the fathers saw their greatest satisfaction as coming from providing a home for a child who might not otherwise have one, and 2% of the mothers saw as the most dissatisfying aspect the fact that they had not had the child from the beginning, that they had not conceived the child themselves.

To get at their attitudes about transracial adoption, attitudes that in many instances might be an expression of their own experiences, each parent was asked during the Time 2 interview to indicate whether in today's climate specific types of transracial adoptions should be encouraged or discouraged. The parents were also provided with the option of checking that they were "not sure." The four types of potential transracial adoptions presented to them were: the adoption by white families of children with two black parents and of children with one black parent, and the adoption by black families of children with two white parents and of children with one white parent. As can be seen from Table 3-7, the responses of the vast majority of both the mothers and the fathers to either white or black families adopting "part-white" or "part-black" children were overwhelmingly favorable. In both instances 91% of the mothers thought such adoption should be encouraged, as did a slightly lower proportion of the fathers. The parents had more reservations and more uncertainty about the two other types of adoption, however. Approximately two-thirds of the mothers and fathers thought there should be encouragement of white families adopting children who have two black parents, and only about three-fifths thought that adoption by black families of children having two white parents should be encouraged.

Table 3-7

Parental Convictions About Transracial Adoptions

	Mothers (N=108)			Fathers (N=103-104)		
	En-courage %	Unsure %	Dis-courage %	En-courage %	Unsure %	Dis-courage %
Whites adopting all-black children	65	25	10	67	23	10
Blacks adopting all-white children	59	27	14	61	27	12
Whites adopting part-black children	91	8	1	87	12	1
Blacks adopting part-white children	91	8	1	83	14	3

Summary

The adoptive parents were motivated to adopt a child by a range of reasons, most often their infertility or inability to have more children. Many had not sought a black child initially, but concern about the need for homes for black children coupled with unavailability of healthy white children led them to this decision. They had some reservations about this, most often because of their family's attitude or because they were not sure a black child would be happy with white parents.

These parents would have been willing to consider a child of almost any racial background, but many would have had serious reservations about adopting a child over 8 years old or one with intellectual or physical handicaps.

A large majority of the parents appeared well satisfied with their experience with the adoption agency. More often than not their preferences about the characteristics of the child to be placed with them were explored by the worker, and these preferences were usually respected. Despite the general positive response, a substantial majority felt they had not received sufficient information about the child's medical history and experience before placement.

As in most adoption studies, the reaction to the adoption experience was overwhelmingly that of satisfaction. Not only did they enjoy the child as a person and companionship with her or him, but they ascribed to the adoption a variety of other benefits, such as enrichment of their marriage.

Within this generally positive picture there were, of course, families who were disappointed or dissatisfied. In subsequent chapters, we explore factors associated with different degrees of parental satisfaction, as well as with other outcome indices.

Chapter 4

OUTCOME MEASURES: THE PROBLEM OF DEFINING SUCCESS

This study of black children adopted by white parents shares
the common problem of adoption studies--indeed, of most studies
of social programs--that of identifying a valid, operational definition of "success." In an ideal society all adopted children,
like their biological peers, would have a happy childhood and
develop into well-adjusted, well-functioning adults. In a much-
less-than-ideal society, it is evident that many, like their biological peers, will not. Since they do not all become "successful"
adults, a series of difficult, usually unanswerable, questions is
raised. Is the failure necessarily related to the fact of adoption?
Is the rate of failure any different from that observed in the
rearing of children by their biological parents? Are the problems
of rearing adopted children essentially those inherent in the
child-rearing process and subject to the same risks or are they
greater? In the specific type of adoption under scrutiny here,
is a black child more "successful" in a white adoptive home than
he would have been in a black foster home or a series of them?

Since humanitarian considerations prohibit deliberate experi-
mentation with any process as crucial as adoption, there are few
ways of demonstrating conclusively that any adopted child is better
off than his counterpart reared by an unmarried mother, by relatives,

or in foster care. Since one cannot produce data about hypothetical situations, the practitioners and the policy-makers who must deal with this question are left with no option other than describing children who have been adopted and assuming that, if they are functioning well in relation to their adoptive families, in school, with their peers, are developing normally, are healthy and reasonably free of symptoms of emotional disturbance, the adoption may be characterized as successful.

Such assessment obviously requires considerable information in a variety of areas and from diverse sources. In this respect, adoption studies also share the dilemmas of child-rearing studies. It is usually not until well into adolescence that children can give valid information about themselves. Their parents, usually the persons best informed about their behavior, are also the most emotionally involved and usually the most biased in their favor. Paper-and-pencil personality tests, which require reading and writing ability on the part of the children, are often not standardized or validated. Tests administered by psychologists and psychiatric evaluations make heavy demands on the research budget, produce more resistance in respondents and also have questionable validity. Seemingly neutral sources of information--case records, social workers' reports, and teachers' evaluations--all have inherent biases and limitations.

Earlier adoption studies have met the problem of defining and measuring outcome in a number of ways. Kadushin summarized 11 adoption studies carried out between 1924 and 1957. The method of data collection most commonly used was that of interviews with the parents (six studies), followed by psychological testing and reviews of case records (five each). Only two used interview materials gathered from third parties. Only one used interviews with adoptees, and one used direct observation of children in the home. Seven of the 11 studies used more than one method.[1]

Of studies involving white inracial adoption published more recently, one "used case records, interviews with adoptive families, casework judgments, psychological evaluations of the adoptees, interviews with the child, peer ratings, evaluations of the child by schools and teacher."[2] Another studied adult adoptees by using case records and interviews with adoptive parents and adoptees.[3]

Four recent studies are more directly comparable with the present study because they dealt, as this one did, with atypical adoptions. Nordlie and Reed reported a followup study of racially mixed children, using a questionnaire directed to case workers at the adoption agency.[4] Welter compared older Japanese adoptees with older

1. Alfred Kadushin, Child Welfare Services. New York: MacMillan, 1967, p. 482.

2. Elizabeth A. Lawder, Katherine D. Lower, Roberta G. Andrews, Edmund A. Sherman and John G. Hill, A Followup Study of Adoptions: Post-Placement Functioning of Adoption Families. New York: Child Welfare League of America, 1969, p. 40.

3. Benson Jaffee and David Fanshel, How They Fared in Adoption. New York: Columbia University Press, 1970.

4. Esther Nordlie and Sheldon Reed, "Followup Adoption Counseling for Children of Possible Racial Admixture," Child Welfare, Vol. 41, No. 7, September 1962, p. 299.

American adoptees through the use of questionnaires directed to caseworkers.[5] Kadushin, studying older white children, used case records and interviews with parents.[6] Fanshel, in a longitudinal study of Indian children, used a series of interviews with adoptive parents.[7]

The specific outcome measures employed by these studies reflect the level of development characteristic of research at the time, and the available technology. Of the early studies summarized by Kadushin, one used the combined judgments of two researchers as to whether the child was "capable" or "incapable" as an adult and two utilized direct statements by the parents on the extent to which they were satisfied with the adoption. Another used the combined judgments of three caseworkers. One used IQ changes; another used removal from the home as its criterion for failure.[8]

Studies reported in the late 1950s reflected an increasing awareness of bias and unreliability in the judgments of interested parties. In these, detailed histories were collected through case

5. Marianne Welter, Comparison of Adopted Older Foreign and American Children. Unpublished doctoral dissertation, Western Reserve University, 1965.

6. Alfred Kadushin, Adopting Older Children. New York: Columbia University Press, 1970.

7. David Fanshel, Far from the Reservation: The Transracial Adoption of American Indian Children. Metuchen, N.J.: Scarecrow Press, 1972.

8. Kadushin, op. cit., pp. 482-483.

records and interviews with parents or a combination of the two. Trained research staff evaluated the data and assigned ratings reflecting relative success to each case.[9]

Studies reported since Kadushin's summary reflect the advances made possible by the use of computers, in which considerable data from a number of sources can be handled. A variety of analytic devices identify various clusters of items that, when taken together, can be seen as a measure of overall success or failure and also produce a series of specific indices that reflect different dimensions of success. Jaffee and Fanshel developed 12 indices of adoptees' adjustment that reflected school performance, personality, past parent-adoptee relationships, social relationships, health, current relationships, economic adjustment, vocational history, heterosexual relations, limitations and social deviations, parents' satisfaction, and talents.[10] Lawder and her colleagues made a global rating of the family's functioning and also analyzed six different aspects of this rating.[11] To measure the adjustment of the children in their study, they used the California Test of Personality, the Minnesota Measure of Mental Ability, the TAT, the Iowa Test of Basic Skills, and the child's self-report of feelings about the adoption and the

---

9. Ibid.

10. Jaffee and Fanshel, op. cit., pp. 220-221.

11. Lawder, et al., op. cit., Chapter 6.

future.[12] Whatever the specific methods involved, these techniques are based on the assumption that their reliability is superior to that of any single rating or judgment.

Outcome Measures

The outcome measures developed for this study also exploited the possibilities created by the use of computers in which a broad array of different types of data could be used to define different forms of outcome. The scores on each form of success could then be combined to make an overall index of "successful placement." The data collection instruments were reviewed for all variables that could be defined as indicators of some aspect of success. These were grouped by conceptual similarity. The correlational analysis program in Harvard Data-Text,[13] which uses the Pearson r, was applied to each group of variables. The items with the highest statistically significant intercorrelations composed each index. In addition to these indices or composite measures, test scores and selected individual responses to key questions were treated as outcome measures. The 15 outcome measures used in the final analysis were grouped as follows:

12. Janet L. Hoopes, Edmund A. Sherman, Elizabeth A. Lawder, Roberta G. Andrews and Katherine D. Lower, A Followup Study of Adoptions (Vol. II): Post-Placement Functioning of Adopted Children. New York: Child Welfare League of America, 1970, pp. 41-50.

13. David Armor and Arthur Couch, Data-Text Primer: An Introduction to Computerized Social Data Analysis. New York: Free Press, 1972, p. 71.

Measures of the Child's Adjustment

1. The child's personal adjustment score on the California Test of Personality.

2. The child's social adjustment score on the California Test of Personality.[14]

3. The child's aggression score on the Missouri Children's Behavior Checklist.

4. The child's inhibition score on the Missouri Children's Behavior Checklist.[15]

Symptoms

A list of symptoms whose presence or absence in the child was reported by the parents yielded three measures:

5. A total symptom score.

6. A physical symptoms index of three related items: colds, headaches, and tiredness.

7. A neurotic symptoms index of three related items: restlessness, bedwetting, and nightmares.

Adult Evaluations

8. Interviewer ratings at Time 1. These covered the following:

   a. Parents' relationship to each other.

   b. Father's relationship to child.

   c. Mother's relationship to child.

   d. Father's relationship to other children in the family.

   e. Mother's relationship to other children in the family.

---

14. The total adjustment score was also obtained, but it was so closely correlated with the personal adjustment score that its use in the analysis would have been an unnecessary duplication of effort.

15. The Missouri Children's Behavior Checklist also scores the children for level of activity and degree of sociability, but the range of scores on these measures was too limited to be useful analytically.

9. Interviewer ratings at Time 2. These covered the following:

   a. Father's acceptance of the child.

   b. Mother's acceptance of the child.

   c. Father's acknowledgment of child's being black.

   d. Mother's acknowledgment of child's being black.

   e. Parents' feeling tone when responding to race-related questions.

   f. Assessment of whether there would be a problem for the child because of racial differences from parents.

   g. Impression of how the adoption has worked out to date.

10. Teacher's Evaluation Index, which summarized the teacher's assessment of the child in relation to:

    a. Academic achievement.

    b. Interest in school work.

    c. Curiosity.

    d. Creativity.

    e. Classroom behavior.

    f. Behavior during recess.

    g. Class relations.

    h. Teacher relations.

11. Parental satisfactions at Time 1. This was an index consisting of eight responses obtained in the Time 1 joint interview and in the individual questionnaires, with the following content:

    a. The mother's statement on how easy or hard it was to rear the study child.

    b. The equivalent statement from the father.

    c. The parents' assessment of the study child's school performance.

d. The mother's statement of the degree of satisfaction derived from the adoption.

e. The equivalent statement from the father.

f. The mother's statement on whether the adoption had enabled her to express deep love.

g. The mother's statement about the effect of the adoption on her marriage.

h. The equivalent statement from the father.

Peer Relations

12. Sibling relations. This index was made up of the parents' assessments of:

a. The child's ability to get along with his siblings.

b. The child's feelings about the siblings.

c. The siblings' feelings about the child.

13. Child relations. This index consisted of four statements by the parents about:

a. The child's ability to get along with children in general.

b. The child's ability to get along with younger children.

c. His ability to get along with older children.

d. His popularity.

Child's Attitude Toward Race

14. Parents' report at Time 1 as to whether the child showed any discomfort about his appearance (as being different from that of the parents).

15. Parents' report at Time 2 on the child's attitude toward his black heritage.

Outcome: Findings

Overall Success

As was indicated earlier, the score for each of these specific forms of outcome was obtained and then a summary score was computed, which was the mean of outcome scores.[16] Since not all the data were obtained for all respondents and the measures used did not have uniform categories, the values were equalized through the use of the T score, which has a standardized mean of 50.[17] For analytic purposes, respondents were divided equally into five categories comprising those whose scores were high, above-average, average, below-average, and low.

A key finding in an adoption study is the number of cases that could be considered "failures" or near failures with a questionable future. None of the families in the study could be classed as a failure by the most extreme criterion, that is, the return of the child to the agency. The possibility of including such cases was probably eliminated by the definition of the sample to include only children who had been in their adoptive homes for 3 years or more. The unusual instances of children returned to agencies from adoptive placements are more likely to occur before legal adoption.

An initial review of the 20% of the sample with the lowest scores indicated that inclusion in this category did not necessarily reflect failure, even though it did reflect a degree of difficulty

---

16. In computing the summary score, four Time 2 scores for parental satisfaction, total symptoms, physical symptoms and neurotic symptoms were also used, but these were not found to be useful in further analysis and are therefore not reported in detail.

17. Armor and Couch, op. cit., p. 42.

greater than that experienced by most of the families in the sample.
Some families had more difficulty than most because, in addition to
the racial element in the adoption, their children had physical
handicaps, learning disabilities, were mentally retarded or had
pre-existing emotional disturbances. Some of these families, however, seemed to be coping adequately with the child's problems so
that these adoptions, far from being failures, might be considered
more than usually successful in light of the obstacles dealt with
initially. In other instances, the low mean score was related to
low test scores or to a higher than usual number of symptoms, without evidence in the interview material of major problems. The low
scores might have been the result of chance errors in the test process or might suggest some latent problem. Without stronger evidence, however, it did not, seem appropriate to classify these
families as failures.

For these reasons, a detailed review of 45 cases of families
whose scores were relatively low was undertaken by the senior
investigators in an attempt to assess whether the family could be
viewed as having serious trouble. Of the cases reviewed, 16 were
judged by the investigators as not appropriate for a list of
families "in trouble." One of the adoptees, for example, was a
hyperactive child who had a difficult adjustment period, suffering
from separation anxiety, but was in a special program in school
and was improving when his parents were interviewed for the second
time. Another was a girl who had been a foster child in the adoptive family and was adopted to prevent "being pushed around." She

was very limited in her school performance, but the parents considered her easy to rear and there was no major evidence of disturbance on the part of the child or of inability to cope on the part of the parents. In another instance, the adoptive parents had been divorced and the mother was having considerable financial difficulty at the time of the first interview. The study child had to repeat kindergarten. By the time of the second interview, the mother had remarried, the whole family was reported to be happier, and the child was doing much better in school.

Twenty-nine cases were identified on which the investigators agreed that the child and the family were in serious difficulties. Examples of these include that of an adolescent girl whose relationship with her mother was so strained that she had dropped out of school and left home. The adoptive father had died several years earlier and the mother had major health problems. Another case involved a boy who presented severe behavior problems, including stealing, and was uninterested in school. At the time of the second interview, his behavior had deteriorated to the point of suspension from school. The parents had a strong tendency to deny the importance of the child's racial background and at the age of 14, he still had not been told that his biological father was black.

Still another child in this category of serious difficulties was a 7-year-old boy described as hyperactive and known to be retarded at the time of placement. By the second interview, the parents acknowledged even more problems than they had in the first interview, saying that they were in constant contact with the

school because of his slowness and his behavior problems. They
also showed a strong denial pattern in relation to his racial
background. They were very defensive and made an unusually negative impression on the interviewer. Another child, an 11-year-old
boy, was known to be severely disturbed at the time of his adoptive
placement at the age of $4\frac{1}{2}$. He did not improve after placement
and at the time of the first interview was in a residential treatment center. At the time of the second interview, he had returned
home but was still having major difficulties. His biological
brother, placed with him, had done well with this family. This
was one of several instances in which the study child was in
difficulty, while other black adopted children appeared to be
doing well. Some parents expressed an understandable resentment
that the study had chosen the difficult child as a subject rather
than those who represented more successful placements. The reverse
situation occurred with families in which the study child was
reported to be doing well, while a sibling, sometimes adopted,
sometimes biological, was described as the family "problem."

Of the 29 families in the "problem" category, a number had
suffered unanticipated catastrophes. In two instances, the adoptive father had died. Two involved serious health problems
developed by the parents after the adoption. Two adoptive couples
were divorced. Nine cases were complicated by the child's physical and intellectual handicaps, which were not being handled as
successfully as by the parents of other children with similar
handicaps.

In 13 of the families in trouble, there was little or no evidence that the child's racial identity was a contributing factor to the problem, which might just as easily have developed in the case of a white adoptee or a biological child. In the other 16, however, there was evidence that problems concerning race were at least part of the total problem and, in some instances, the central problems. In two of these families, the parents had apparently been extremely naive about the racial aspects of the adoption. In both instances, the study child had been placed for foster care in infancy. The foster parents had decided to adopt rather than risk giving up the child, apparently without anticipating the impact the racial difference would have as he grew older. In nine cases, there was evidence that the child was in some conflict about his racial identity and his parents were having difficulty in dealing with it. In the remaining five cases, the parents showed a strong tendency to deny the child's racial background by minimizing its importance or passively ignoring it. This was sometimes justified by the child's fair appearance or by lack of specific information about his background. In a few extreme cases, children with a clearly Negroid appearance had not been told of their adoption or their black biological parentage.

Comparisons With Other Studies

The decision that 29 of the 125 families in the sample (23%) were in serious trouble gives the sample an overall "success" rate of 77%. This finding can be compared with those studies noted earlier in which an overall rate is given or can be deduced from the data reported.

Table 4-1

Comparison of Success Rate

	%
Summarized rate for 11 studies of white infant adoption[18]	78
Racially mixed[19]	72
Japanese[20]	89
Older white[21]	73-78
Indian children[22]	88

Thus, the finding in this study that 77% of the adoptions of black children by white parents could be considered successful indicates a level of success approximately the same as that obtained in other adoption studies, both for traditional white infant adoptions and nontraditional adoptions involving racial mixtures and older children.

---

18. Kadushin, Child Welfare Service, op. cit., p. 483.

19. Nordlie and Reed, op. cit., p. 304.

20. Welter, op. cit., p. 126.

21. Kadushin, Adopting Older Children, op. cit., p. 63.

22. Fanshel, op. cit., p. 333.

Table 4-2

Types of Outcome and Their Frequency Distributions

Measure	N	Categories	%	"Success" rate*
1. Social Adjustment Score, California Test of Personality	113	Low (1st-30th percentile) Average (40th-60th) High (70th-99th)	40 33 27	60%
2. Personal Adjustment Score, CTP	113	Low (1st-30th) Average (40th-60th) High (70th-99th)	32 47 21	68%
3. Aggression Score, Missouri Children's Behavior Checklist	124**	Moderate aggression (5-17) Slight aggression (2-4) Unaggressive (0-1)	31 34 35	69%
4. Inhibition Score, Missouri Children's Behavior Checklist	124	Inhibited (4-8) Somewhat inhibited (2-3) Uninhibited (0-1)	17 35 48	83%
5. Total Symptom Score	125	Moderate-high (6-12) Minimal-free (0-5)	46 54	54%
6. Physical Symptom Score	125	Some symptoms Slight symptoms Symptom-free	24 38 38	76%
7. Neurotic Symptom Score	125	Some symptoms Slight symptoms Symptom-free	24 30 46	76%
8. Interviewer's Evaluation--Family Relations	125	Not warm Warm Very warm	28 43 29	72%
9. Interviewer's Evaluation--Racial Attitudes	114	Somewhat negative Positive Very positive	33 41 26	67%
10. Teacher's Evaluation	92	Poorer than others Like others Better than others	33 36 31	67%
11. Parental Satisfaction--Time 1	125	Mixed Positive Very positive	34 32 34	66%

* The "success" rate is a combination of the two highest categories in a three-category scale or the higher category in a two-category scale.

** Both parents gave data for this test, but only the mother's was used in the analysis. Since data for one child were given only by the father, this case was not used.

Table 4-2 (Continued)

	Measure	N	Categories		"Success" Rate
12.	Sibling Relations	120*	Problematic Good Very good	22 42 36	78%
13.	Relations With Children	125	Problematic Good Very good	16 45 39	84%
14.	Discomfort About Appearance	125	Uncomfortable No discomfort	32 68	68%
15.	Attitude Toward Black Heritage	115	Confused/negative Unknown/neutral Positive	24 44 32	76%

*   Five children had no siblings.

Table 4-3 Intercorrelations of Outcome Measures Significant at or Beyond .05 Level

Outcome Measure	1	2	3	4	5	6	7	8	9	10	11	12	13	14	15
1. Personal Adjustment Score	X	.58	.20	--	--	--	--	--	--	--	.27	--	--	--	--
2. Social Adjustment Score		X	.30	--	--	--	--	--	--	--	.24	.26	.26	--	--
3. Aggression			X	.19	.22	--	.33	.32	--	--	.57	.39	--	.21	--
4. Inhibition				X	.22	--	.27	--	--	--	.19	--	--	--	--
5. Total Symptoms					X	.50	.65	--	--	.34	--	--	--	--	--
6. Physical Symptoms						X	--	--	--	--	--	--	--	--	--
7. Neurotic Symptoms							X	--	--	.41	.28	.24	--	--	--
8. Interviewer Evaluation—Family								X	.40	--	.26	.19	--	--	.20
9. Interviewer Evaluation—Racial Attitudes									X	--	--	--	.20	--	--
10. Teacher Evaluation										X	.22	--	--	--	--
11. Parental Satisfaction											X	.21	.19	.21	--
12. Sibling Relations												X	--	.24	--
13. Child Relations													X	--	--
14. Discomfort About Appearance														X	--
15. Attitude Toward Black Heritage															X

Specific Outcomes: Findings

The success rates for each defintion of success reflected in the indices have a range of 30 percentage points, from 54% to 84%. Most of the rates are between 66% and 76%, so that one can infer that, by most criteria, from two-thirds to three-quarters of the adoptions in the sample are successful. Table 4-2 illustrates these findings.

These 15 measures are clearly interrelated and overlapping. Through them, outcome is examined from different vantage points and at different times. Our first concern was whether they overlapped to such a degree that a smaller number would suffice equally well. To judge this, the correlation of each outcome measure with every other outcome measure was computed. Of 105 correlations, 33 were statistically significant, that is, the measures showed a better-than-chance relation to each other in 31% of the comparisons. However, most of the correlations were relatively low, with only three reaching a figure as high as .50 and the highest being .65. Only if a correlation reaches .80 can as many as two-thirds of the ratings on one measure be predicted from the other, and the two regarded as redundant. Therefore, all the indices were retained. The correlations that were statistically significant are shown in Table 4-3. The patterning is expectable in many instances; for example, relatively high correlations of physical and neurotic symptom scores with total symptom scores, and significant though modest correlations of several other indices with parental satisfaction. On the other hand, neither measure of the child's attitude toward race is related to any of the measures of his overall adjustment.

Correlates of Success

Each of the outcome measures was examined in relation to 55 of the independent variables to try to identify factors predictive of successful adoption. These variables included demographic and social characteristics of the child and of the adoptive parents, the parents' adoption experience, their life styles, their attitudes on race, and characteristics of the communities where they live. With a few exceptions, each of the independent variables showed a significant relationship (as measured by the chi-square test) with at least one of the outcome measures, but no one of them was consistently related to all or even a majority of the outcome measures. This stage of the analysis yielded many surprises. For example, the age of the child at placement was associated with only one outcome measure, the child's attitude toward his black heritage. Whether the child was obviously black was associated with some outcome measures, but not with any of the child's test scores or with his attitude toward his heritage.

When groups of variables showing a significant relation to a particular outcome measure were examined in combination, through regression analysis, several of these were found to have no predictive value if the other related items were held constant.

Thus, within this small and relatively homogeneous sample no clear patterns emerged of factors strongly predictive of success from the various vantage points from which we viewed it. Since the factors related to success by one criterion were not necessarily those related to it by another, we discuss, in subsequent chapters, the findings for each group of outcome measures in the belief that these findings will be at least suggestive of factors that play a role in some form of success.

In light of the foregoing, it is not surprising that, when the outcome measures were brought together in a summary score, only two relationships with the independent variables were statistically significant. These were the parents' perception of the child's blackness, and the size of the family.

Perception of Blackness

During the second interview parents were asked whether the child was "obviously black." As was stated in Chapter 2, 55% of the parents replied in the affirmative, while 45% thought the child's racial origins were not obvious. Some of these responses were not entirely consistent with data collected in the first interview, in which parents were asked to describe the child's skin color and to indicate whether or not he had other Negroid features. The information given was combined in the coding process and the children were classified as 1) fair-skinned with no Negroid features, 2) light brown skin with no Negroid features, 3) fair-skinned with Negroid features, 4) light brown skin with Negroid features, 5) dark brown skin with Negroid features. The relation between responses to these two questions is seen in Table 4-4.

Table 4-4

Appearance of the Child (Time 1) and Perception of Parents (Time 2)

Description of Appearance	Parents' Perception	
	Obviously Black	Not Obviously Black
Fair/no Negroid features	1	18
Light brown/no Negroid features	12	13
Fair/Negroid features	2	10
Light brown/Negroid features	36	9
Dark brown/Negroid features	11	1
Total	62	51

This table indicates that 15 children who were relatively light were described by their parents as "obviously black," while 10 children with brown skin and Negroid features were described by their parents as not obviously black. Thus for 25 children, or 20% of the sample, there seems to be some misperception or inconsistency on the parents' part. It is also noteworthy that the 25 children described as having light brown skin with no Negroid features were evenly divided between those whose parents thought they were obviously black and those who thought they were not.

When the parents' perception of blackness was related to the summary outcome score, the findings indicated that children designated as obviously black were more likely to have average or high scores than were those whose parents felt they were not obviously black.

Table 4-5

Summary Scores and Parents' Perception of Blackness

Summary Score	Obviously Black (N=62) %	Not Obvious (N=51) %
Below average	31	53
Average/above	69	47
	—	—
Total	100	100

Chi-square = 4.88, df 1, p < .05

When the parents' Time 1 description of the child's appearance is related to the summary score, no such relationship is seen. In fact, the proportions of average and high scores are almost identical: 60% of the lighter children have such scores, as do 59% of the darker children. Thus it appears that it is not the parents' description of the child that is related to his overall adjustment, but their perception of his blackness as "obvious." A regression analysis indicated that the parents' perception of blackness as "obvious" accounted for 7% of the variance in the summary index scores, while the description of his appearance accounted for only 2%. When both variables are entered into the same equation, the relationship between the parents' perception of "obvious" blackness and the summary scores is statistically significant while the description is not.

Since this perception of the child's appearance as "obviously" black proved important, other evidence on this point was also examined. At Time 2, interviewers were asked to describe, for

-111-

those children whom they saw at Time 2 or remembered from Time 1, the color of their skin and whether they had Negroid features. Table 4-6 compares the frequency distributions obtained through the interviewers' observations with those obtained from the parents who were interviewed at Time 1.

Table 4-6

Interviewers' and Parents' Descriptions
of Study Children

	Parents' Descriptions (N=113) %	Interviewers' Descriptions (N=98) %
Fair/no Negroid features	17	13
Light brown/no Negroid features	22	8
Fair/Negroid features	11	12
Light brown/Negroid features	40	49
Dark brown/Negroid features	10	18
Total	100	100

If the first three categories representing the lighter children are combined, it is evident that 50% of the children are seen by their parents as relatively light, but only 33% are so described by the interviewers. Cross-tabulations of parents' descriptions against interviewers' descriptions indicated that about 75% of their statements were compatible. For the remainder, in which they disagreed, usually the parents saw their children as lighter than did the interviewers. Only 3% of the parents saw their children as having Negroid features when the interviewers did not, in contrast to 21% who did not see their children as Negroid when the interviewers did.

For this study, it was not practical to separate analytically those cases where there was evidence of misperception. The importance of this factor, however, needs to be kept in mind since, as the reader will see in subsequent chapters, the parents' descriptions of the child's appearance and their perception of his blackness as obvious are important variables in relation to several different forms of outcome.

Size of Family

One other variable showed a statistically significant relationship, but its substantive significance is more limited. The analysis indicated that children in the largest family units, those having five or more children, were significantly less likely than children in smaller family units to have low scores.

Table 4-7

Summary Scores and Large Families

	1-4 Children (N=93) %	5 or more (N=32) %
Below average	46	22
Average/above	54	78
	—	—
Total	100	100

Chi-square = 4.92, 1 df, $p < .05$

The difference, it should be noted, is not a linear one; it does not imply that the larger the family, the better adjusted the child. The study children living with two or three siblings were not necessarily better off than those who were only children or who had one sibling. It is only when the largest family units are compared with the rest of the sample that the difference appears.

Summary

The success of transracial adoption was assessed in this study by a series of 15 measures, including test scores, indices developed from different types of data supplied by the parents, teachers' evaluations, and interviewer ratings. The scores on these measures were combined in a single score to measure overall success.

The findings indicate that 77% of the adoptions may be seen as successful. This rate is approximately the same as that of other studies that have examined conventional white infant adoptions, as well as those concerned with adoption of older children and other racial groups.

An examination of the relationship between the summary score and variables describing the family and child indicates that only two are statistically significant. Children perceived by their parents as "obviously black" were more likely to have higher summary scores than those whose blackness was perceived as not obvious. Children in the largest family units (five or more children) were also likely to have higher scores than those in smaller units.

Chapter 5

SUCCESS AS MEASURED BY TEST SCORES

Of the various types of outcome measures available in this
study, the most objective are the results of the California Test
of Personality. Since the test was administered to the child
directly, it can be assumed to be relatively uninfluenced by the
parents' bias. The Missouri Children's Behavior Checklist, which
was incorporated in a questionnaire addressed to the parents,
consists of a series of descriptive statements that yield an
assessment of the extent to which a child may be excessively
aggressive or excessively inhibited. Since the parents supply
the information, some bias in the form of understatement of problems may be expected, but the data obtained are in any case less
subjective than the parents' more general assessments of the
child's behavior.

The California Test of Personality has two components: a
personal adjustment score and a social adjustment score. They
may be combined into a total adjustment score. For this sample,
it was noted that the children tested showed a sufficiently higher
proportion of low (1st to 30th percentile) scorers (40%) on the
social adjustment measure than on the personal adjustment measure
(32%) to warrant a separate analysis of the two subscores. Both
sets of test results showed significant relationships with some

independent variables, but the patterns were different for the two measures. (Low scores imply unfavorable performance on the test.)

This chapter examines the correlates of successful adoption as measured by the personal adjustment scores and the social adjustment scores of the CTP, and then examines the correlates of aggression and inhibition as measured by the Missouri Children's Behavior Checklist.

Personal Adjustment Scores

The personal adjustment score is designed to reflect a group of tendencies to "feel, think, and act," including self-reliance ("can do things independently of others, depend upon himself in various situations, and direct his own activities"), sense of personal worth ("feels well regarded by others. . . has average or better than average ability, feels capable, and reasonably attractive"), sense of personal freedom ("permitted to have a reasonable share in the determination of his conduct and in setting the general policies that shall govern his life. . . permission to choose own friends and have a little spending money"), feeling of belonging ("enjoys love of family, well wishes of good friends and cordial relationships with people in general"), withdrawing tendencies ("substitutes joys of a fantasy world for actual success in real life. . . sensitive, lonely, given to self-concern"), nervous symptoms (". . . loss of appetite. . . frequent eye strain, inability to sleep").[1]

---

1. <u>Manual</u>, California Test of Personality, California Test Bureau, McGraw-Hill, 1953, p. 3.

Although the personal adjustment scores for the study children who took the test had a reasonably normal distribution, these scores showed statistically significant relationships with two of the independent variables.

Time in Placement

Children who had been in their adoptive placement for 3 to 4 years, the shortest period possible by the definition of the study sample, were significantly more likely to have low scores than children who had been in their homes longer.

Table 5-1[2]

Personal Adjustment Scores and Years in Placement

Score	3-4 Years (N=18) %	5-8 Years (N=70) %	9 or More (N=25) %
Low	50	27	32
Average	50	51	32
High	0	22	36
Total	100	100	100

Chi-square = 10.26, 4 df, p < .05

As the reader will see, this pattern, in which the children with the least time in placement show signs of greater difficulties than those in placement longer, recurs with several other outcome variables. It is not in itself surprising, but suggests that the

2. In this and subsequent chapters except Chapter 10, tables are presented only for variables that accounted for a statistically significant proportion of the variance in the regression analysis. Thus the items reported are those that retain their influence on the dependent variable when other variables are controlled.

adjustment of these children is a slow process and that it is only after the fourth year of placement that a more normal pattern for the group as a whole begins to appear. It is somewhat surprising that the group longest in care has such a high proportion of high scores, since they are in or approaching adolescence and since other outcome scores, discussed later, suggest problems in the oldest children.

Religion and Church Attendance

The only other factor associated with low personal adjustment scores is the mother's religion.[3] Most respondents, as noted in Chapter 2, were Protestants or Catholics, but a small number professed a minority affiliation or none at all. Children in Protestant or Catholic families did not differ from each other in relation to the personal adjustment scores, but those in minority religions or unaffiliated had a disproportionately high number of children whose scores were low.

The personal adjustment scores are the only form of outcome related to religious affiliation. In other instances in which religion is a factor, it is church attendance, not the affiliation, that is important.

When the mother's church attendance is related to the personal adjustment score, 42% of the children of those who attend irregularly have low scores, in contrast to 27% of the children whose mothers

---

3. Mother's religion was used in this analysis because there were more mothers than fathers in the study. In nearly all instances the mother's religion was also the father's religion.

attend regularly. The difference, however, misses statistical

significance at the .05 level.

Table 5-2

Personal Adjustment Scores and Mother's Religion

Score	Protestants-Catholics (N=92) %	Minority-Unaffiliated (N=21) %
Low	26	57
Average	49	38
High	25	5
	—	—
Total	100	100

Chi-square = 8.90, 2 df, p < .01

Social Adjustment Scores

The social adjustment scores measure six tendencies: 1) social

standards ("understands rights of others and appreciates necessity

of subordinating certain desires to the needs of the group. . .

understands what is regarded as being right or wrong"), 2) social

skill ("subordinates his or her egotistic tendencies in favor of

interest in the problems and activities of his associates"),

3) antisocial tendencies ("given to bullying, frequent quarreling,

disobedience and destructiveness to property"), 4) family relations

("feels loved and well-treated at home, has a sense of security and

self-respect"), 5) school relations ("feels his teachers like him,

enjoys being with other students, finds school work adapted to his

level of interest and maturity"), 6) community relations ("mingles happily with neighbors, takes pride in community improvements, tolerant in dealing with strangers and foreigners").[4]

As indicated earlier, a disproportionately high number of study children showed more than usual difficulty in the area of social adjustment. In contrast to the few independent variables that were associated with the personal adjustment scores, on social adjustment scores significant relationships were found with eight independent variables and near-significant relationships with two others. Since some were obviously interrelated, a regression analysis was done; it indicated that five of the eight variables accounted for a statistically significant portion of the variance even when the other variables were controlled.

Length of Time in Placement

As was the case with the personal adjustment scores, the children in their adoptive homes for 3 or 4 years have a much higher proportion of low scorers than any other group, even higher than was seen on the personal adjustment scores. The pattern for children in care longer is more puzzling, since the relationship is not linear. Children in placement 5 to 8 years have a fairly even distribution among the three categories, while those in placement 9 or more have a relatively large proportion of low scores.

---

4. Manual, California Test of Personality, op. cit., pp. 3-4.

Table 5-3

Years in Placement and Social Adjustment Scores

Score	3-4 Years (N=18) %	5-8 Years (N=70) %	9 or more (N=25) %
Low	72	28	48
Average	11	39	32
High	17	33	20
Total	100	100	100

Chi-square = 12.71, 4 df, p < .02

It is worth noting that the influential variable is the time in placement, not the age of the child. When the relationship between test scores and age is examined, no such trends are seen. Neither is the child's age at placement related to personal or social adjustment.

Income

Another variable related to the social adjustment score is income, but again the relationship is not linear. As Table 5-4 indicates, families in the middle-income range for this sample have a much smaller proportion of children among the low scorers than either the lowest or the highest income groups.

This is a somewhat surprising finding. The respondents were widely scattered over the North American continent, where dollar incomes vary in their significance. Fifteen thousand may be a high income in some areas and average in others. The sample is also of a limited socioeconomic range, as compared with the general population. For this reason and because no means were found of standardizing these income figures, income was not expected to relate significantly to any of the outcome measures. In fact, income was related to only one other outcome and in the same bi-modal way.

Table 5-4

Social Adjustment Scores and Income

Score	Under $15,000 (N=52) %	$15-19,999 (N=26) %	$20,000 or More (N=35) %
Low	46	15	49
Average/high	54	85	51
Total	100	100	100

Chi-square = 8.47, 2 df, p < .02

Perhaps the relative difference rather than the actual figures reflects other problems. The lowest income group includes the families who were in financially stressful situations that could have affected the social adjustment of their children. Why the highest income group also shows an unduly high proportion of children with problems is harder to explain. Perhaps social demands are even greater for black children in the affluent neighborhoods in which these families are likely to be found than the demands are elsewhere.

Reason for Adoption

Another variable that accounts for a significant degree of variance in the social adjustment scores is the reason for adoption. Children of parents who gave infertility as their reason for adoption had a much smaller proportion of low scorers and a larger proportion of average scorers than did those whose parents' motivation was social or other (personal or circumstantial).

This is also a surprising finding, since families whose motivation for adoption is the inability to bear children of their own could be expected to be the ones most likely to want a healthy white infant and to accept a racially mixed or black child only as an alternative to independent adoption or to remaining childless. One would then expect them to have children with greater problems in social adjustment than those whose parents had more direct social motives and who adopted the children they asked for. Instead, the reverse is seen. It should be recalled, however, that, though the study child is the oldest black adoptee, he is not necessarily the first adoptee. For 40 families, the first child or children adopted were white or of another racial mixture. In this group, those unable to have children are overrepresented. It is possible that their greater experience as adoptive parents, together with the possibility that conflicts about infertility had been resolved earlier, is reflected in the better social adjustment of their children. It is possible that the strength of their desire for children made them more ready to accept and nurture a child regardless of his individual characteristics.

Table 5-5

Reason for Adoption and Social Adjustment Scores

Score	Infertility (N=40) %	Social (N=40) %	Other (N=33) %
Low	25	53	42
Average	55	20	21
High	20	27	37
Total	100	100	100

Chi-square = 15.02, 4 df, p < .01

Community Size

The size of the community is also significantly related to the social adjustment scores. A much larger proportion of children living in communities with a population of over 250,000 have average or high scores than of children living in moderate-sized or small communities.

Table 5-6

Social Adjustment Scores and Size of Community

Score	Under 10,000 (N=21) %	10-249,000 (N=66) %	250,000 or Higher (N=26) %
Low	48	47	15
Average/high	52	53	85
Total	100	100	100

Chi-square = 8.42, 2 df, p < .02

This finding may reflect the fact that the largest communities are the ones with the largest black populations, therefore more likely to be centers of black activism, and to have a more liberal white population where socially mixed groups are not unusual.

Mother's Openness to Handicapped Children

As reported in Chapter 3, data from the parents' questionnaire indicated the extent to which each parent was open to the possibility of adopting children handicapped in ways other than their racial origins. The correlational analysis indicated that the mother's statements on openness to the retarded, to children with correctable and with noncorrectable handicaps, and to those with mental illness in the family were so intercorrelated that an index combining all of these responses would reflect the degree of openness to the idea of adopting a handicapped child. The same held true for the father's statements, with the difference that his "openness" also included older children. It is noteworthy that the statements of both were not so highly intercorrelated that they could be combined in an index of family openness; that is, the mother's attitude did not necessarily predict the father's, and vice versa.

When the index scores were computed, the largest group of mothers (41%) indicated openness to the possibility of adoption for most types of handicaps described. About a third were relatively open but expressed some reservations, and the smallest group (27%) had scores indicating that they were not willing to adopt any type of handicapped child. It was thought that the parents' responses to these questions would reflect a degree of openness or receptivity to children in need, the "room for one more" phenomenon, that could bear some relation to the successful adjustment of the study child. In fact, the index reflecting the mother's attitude proves to be related to several forms of outcome. The father's openness was also significantly related to some forms of outcome, although not to so many as the mother's. Both indices present a problem in interpretation, since they can be seen not only as independent variables (attitudes of the parents that could affect success in rearing study children) but as dependent variables (effects of the adoption experience on the parents). Furthermore, the relationships were not always linear. In this case, the mothers with mixed feelings about adopting handicapped children were the ones who had the highest proportion of children showing difficulty in social adjustment. Children with mothers who were clearly open or not open tended to have either average or high scores.

It is possible that a middle-range score on this variable represents some ambivalence or confusion about adoption that may occur concurrently with or be reinforced by the child's poor social adjustment.

Table 5-7

Social Adjustment Scores and Mother's Openness to
the Adoption of the Handicapped

Score	Not Open (N=30) %	Somewhat Open (N=37) %	Open (N=46) %
Low	30	57	33
Average/high	70	43	67
Total	100	100	100

Chi-square = 6.63, 2 df, p < .04

Aggression Scores

Unlike the California Test of Personality, the Missouri
Children's Behavior Checklist is not standardized and it has been
used largely on nonclinical populations. The distribution on both
the aggression and inhibition scores for this study sample were
markedly one-sided. Most of the children were described as totally
unaggressive (35%) or slightly aggressive (34%), and uninhibited
(48%) or slightly inhibited (35%), with only a minority showing
a relatively high degree of aggression or inhibition. These distributions, as well as some of the relationships presented later,
cast some doubt as to whether the test measures aggression in a
nonclinical population, and whether such aggression as is reported
is necessarily seen by the parents in a negative light.

Thirty-eight children, or 31% of the sample, had relatively
high aggression scores. The presence of this unusual degree of
aggression was associated with six variables. Two were demographic
in nature and the others reflected parental attitudes.

Sex

Not surprisingly, boys were somewhat more likely to have high
aggression scores than girls.

This difference could be attributed to the general societal
expectation still prevalent despite the women's liberation movement,
that boys should be more aggressive than girls. However, boys are
also more likely to display physical and neurotic symptoms and to
have lower evaluations by their teachers, as the following chapter
documents. It is possible that the combination of the pressures

of maleness and blackness on the boys leads to more than the normal expression of aggression.

Table 5-8

Aggression Scores and Sex of the Child

Score	Girls (N=60) %	Boys (N=64) %
Unaggressive	35	36
Slightly aggressive	43	25
Moderately aggressive	22	39
Total	100	100

Chi-square = 6.14, 2 df, p < .05

Length of Marriage

Parents married less than 10 years at the time of placement have a markedly higher proportion of children with an unusually high aggression score than those married longer.

This relationship is not explained by the age of the parents, which showed no influence on the aggression score.

Table 5-9

Aggression Scores and Number of Years of Parents' Marriage

Score	Under 10 Years (N=53) %	10-14 Years (N=40) %	15 Years and Over (N=28) %
Unaggressive	28	37	46
Slightly aggressive	27	47	29
Moderately aggressive	45	16	25
Total	100	100	100

Chi-square = 12.02, 4 df, p < .02

Parents' Attitude Toward Blacks

Parents who took the strongest problack positions on the racial attitudes questionnaire also had a disproportionately high number of aggressive children.

Table 5-10

Aggression Scores and Parents' Attitudes
Toward Blacks

Score	Uncertain/ Generally Problack (N=73) %	Strongly Problack (N=40) %
Unaggressive/slightly aggressive	71	53
Moderately aggressive	29	47
Total	100	100

Chi-square = 5.13, 1 df, p < .02

It is possible that militant or strongly felt political attitudes in parents and aggressive behavior on the part of children represent a life style in which taking strong stands, "speaking out," etc., are encouraged.

Father's Permissiveness

On this measure, fathers reporting tendencies to be strict in their child-rearing practices were almost equal in proportion (35%) to those who tended toward permissiveness (37%). Those with middle-range scores, constituting 28% of the respondents, might be seen in positive terms as having achieved a balance between the the two extremes, or negatively as being inconsistent. However, since their children have the largest proportion of high aggression scores, it seems more plausible to infer that a middle-range score on this variable implies inconsistency.

Table 5-11

Aggression Scores and Father's Permissiveness

Score	Middle-Range (N=32) %	Strict/ Permissive (N=81) %
Unaggressive	16	42
Slightly aggressive	44	30
Moderately aggressive	40	28
	—	—
Total	100	100

Chi-square = 7.06, 2 df, p < .05

Mother's Openness to the Handicapped

The mother's score on the index reflecting openness to the handicapped is associated with aggression in the same pattern seen in relation to the social adjustment score. It is the mothers in the middle group who do not have a strong position one way or the other who have the largest proportion of children with high aggression scores.

Interpretation of this finding might be the same as for relationship of this variable with the social adjustment score, presented earlier. An uncertain, in-between position on this question may be related to a more pervasive ambivalence, which could be more disturbing to a child than a clear conviction in either direction.

Table 5-12

Aggression Scores and Mother's Openness
to the Handicapped

Score	Not Open (N=32) %	Somewhat Open (N=38) %	Open (N=54) %
Unaggressive	37	18	47
Slightly aggressive	27	40	34
Moderately aggressive	36	42	19
Total	100	100	100

Chi-square = 10.32, 4 df, p < .04

Satisfaction With Agency Services

It is also worth noting that, on the index reflecting the extent to which parents were satisfied with the services of the adoption agencies, the dissatisfied families had a disproportionately large number of children with high aggression scores.

Table 5-13

Aggression Scores and Parental Satisfaction
with Agency Services

Score	Dissatisfied (N=41) %	Somewhat Dissatisfied (N=39) %	Satisfied (N=44) %
Unaggressive	25	38	43
Slightly aggressive	29	31	41
Moderately aggressive	46	31	16
Total	100	100	100

Chi-square = 9.68, 4 df, p < .05

This relationship, however, raises the question of which is cause and which is effect. Because the parents have an unusually aggressive child, the dissatisfaction they express may be a retrospective evaluation of the agency service rather than a true reflection of their feelings at the time of placement.

Inhibition Scores

The inhibition scores on the Missouri Children's Behavior Checklist were significantly related to three variables.

Child's Appearance

Significantly more of the children at both color extremes, the darkest and the lightest, showed evidence of an unusual degree of inhibition than did those in the middle range.

Table 5-14

Inhibition Scores and Child's Appearance

Score	Fair, No Negroid Features (N=20) %	Light Brown, No Negroid Features (N=26) %	Fair, Negroid Features (N=14) %	Light Brown, Negroid Features (N=51) %	Dark Brown, Negroid Features (N=13) %
Uninhibited	35	50	74	51	23
Slightly/ moderately inhibited	65	50	21	49	77
Total	100	100	100	100	100

Chi-square = 10.04, 4 df, p < .05

The inhibition in the two groups may, of course, appear for different reasons. The possibility of denial, both of adoption and of the child's racial heritage, is greatest in the lightest children and may lead to a degree of inhibition in these children more severe than others. The darkest children, on the other hand, are the ones most clearly different and most conspicuous in the environments in which most of them find themselves, a circumstance that can also be inhibiting.

Parents' Expectations

Parents whose preference in relation to the intellectual potential of the child was not matched have a disproportionately high number of children with scores indicating a relatively high degree of inhibition.

Table 5-15

Inhibition Scores and Unmatched Expectations
on Intellectual Level

Score	No Preferences Expressed (N=63) %	Preferences Matched (N=34) %	Preferences Not Matched (N=27) %
Uninhibited	47	47	52
Slightly inhibited	40	41	15
Moderately inhibited	13	12	33
	—	—	—
Total	100	100	100

Chi-square = 9.52, 4 df, p < .05

It is not surprising that parents whose intellectual preferences were not met should feel some disappointment or strain which,
in turn, is conveyed to their children. This pattern is also
reflected, as is noted later, in the child's physical and neurotic
symptoms. It should be remembered that the mismatching occurred
in both directions; not only did parents who preferred highly
intelligent children receive children of lower intellectual capacity, but a slightly larger number who said they preferred a child
of average intelligence actually received a child of relatively
high intelligence. Thus there may be two kinds of strain here:
the disappointment of parents in children who do not live up to
their intellectual expectations and the strains imposed on those
whose children may be demanding more than the parents are prepared
to give.

Parental Convictions About Transracial Adoption

As indicated in Chapter 3, parents were asked whether they
would or would not encourage four different types of transracial
adoption. Although the overall response was solidly in the direction of encouragement, some parents showed some doubt about totally
transracial adoptions (an all-black child in a white family or a
white child in a black family). On these items, the respondents
were equally divided between those who clearly encouraged such
adoptions and those who had some reservations. The analysis indicated that parents who had such doubts were likely to have a disproportionately large number of children with high scores on the
inhibition measure.

Table 5-16

Inhibition Scores and Convictions About
Totally Transracial Adoptions

Score	Encouragement (N=56) %	Doubts (N=57) %
Uninhibited	48	49
Slightly inhibited	45	25
Moderately inhibited	7	26
Total	100	100

Chi-square = 9.48, 2 df, p < .01

Both the inhibition in the child and the doubts of the parents
may reflect some unaccounted factor, so that the apparent relation
between these two variables may be spurious.

Summary

The four outcome measures derived from personality tests
differed in the descriptive variables to which they were related.
Children with low personal adjustment scores on the California
Test of Personality tended to be those who had been in placement
3 to 4 years, the shortest time period for this sample. They also
tended to be found in families of minority religions or those
unaffiliated with any church. Children with low social adjustment
scores also tended to have been in placement only 3 to 4 years.
Low scores on this measure were also associated with the extremes
of the income scale, with social or personal (other than infertility)
reasons for adoption, with living in small communities, with the
mother's uncertainty or ambivalence about the adoption of the handicapped, and with dissatisfaction with the agency's services.

High aggression scores on the Missouri Children's Behavior Checklist were more likely to be made by boys than by girls, and by children whose adoptive parents had been married less than 10 years. High aggression scores also appeared in children whose parents hold particularly strong "problack" attitudes, in children whose fathers are neither consistently permissive or consistently strict, and, as was the case with the low social adjustment score, in children whose mothers are ambivalent about the adoption of the handicapped.

High inhibition scores ase associated with both very light and very dark appearance, with failure to match the parents' expectation on intellectual preference, and with doubts about the validity of transracial adoption.

Chapter 6

SUCCESS AS MEASURED BY SYMPTOM SCORES

Symptom scores for each study child were developed from
parents' responses when asked to specify the extent to which the
child suffered from each of 12 symptoms commonly associated with
physical and emotional disorders. These symptoms, which parallel
items on the California Test of Personality, included lack of
appetite, colds, fingernail-biting, eyes hurting, sneezing, thumb-
sucking, restlessness, headaches, tiredness, bed-wetting, feeling
sick, nightmares. Each child was assigned a total score on the
symptom list on the assumption that the more symptoms he displayed,
the greater the possibility of an underlying disturbance.

Correlational analysis indicated that two sets of three items
each on this list tended to cluster together. Colds, headaches
and tiredness formed a "physical symptoms" index, while restlessness, bed-wetting and nightmares constituted a "neurotic symptoms"
index. The symptom of restlessness was particularly strongly correlated with negative assessments of the adoption experience by the
parents, as well as with low teacher ratings.

The total symptom scores, the physical symptoms index and the
neurotic symptoms index, based on the initial parent interview,
showed somewhat different patterns of relationships with the independent variables. When the same questions were also asked in the

second interview, fewer of the symptoms included in the two indices were reported. Significant relationships with the independent variables were fewer and weaker but, as is shown later, several patterns observed at Time 1 were also seen at Time 2.

Neurotic Symptoms Index

The neurotic symptoms index seemingly reflects the most serious disturbances among the children. The analysis indicated that five independent variables accounted for a significant degree of variance in the presence or absence of these symptoms. These were the age and sex of the child, the number of children in the home, the age of the mother, and the extent to which the parents' intellectual preferences were matched in the adoption.

Age of the Child

The strongest of these relationships, accounting for 6% of the variance in the neurotic symptoms score, is the age of the child. When children in the oldest group--those over 12--are contrasted to the rest of the sample, they are markedly freer of symptoms than any of the younger children. At the second interview, this relationship is even stronger.

A similar relationship, as would be expected, appears when the neurotic symptoms score is related to the length of time in placement. At the first interview, 62% of the children in place- ment 9 years or more were symptom-free, in contrast to 41% of the rest of the sample. At the second interview, 79% of the children in placement 9 years or longer were symptom-free, in contrast to 50% of the rest of the sample. The age difference, however, has a stronger effect on the neurotic symptoms index than time in placement, a finding in contrast to that reported in Chapter 4 for the social adjustment score, on which higher scores seemed more a function of time than of age. The disappearance of the kinds of symptoms included in this index are most likely the result of developmental processes, and not a function of length of time in adoptive homes.

Table 6-1

Neurotic Symptoms Score and Age of Child

	First Interview			
Score	6-7 (N=48) %	8-9 (N=36) %	10-11 (N=20) %	12 and over (N=20) %
Frequent/occasional symptoms	52	69	52	30
Symptom-free	48	31	48	70
Total	100	100	100	100

Chi-square = 8.17, 3 df, p < .04

	Second Interview			
Score	6-7 (N=19) %	8-9 (N=48) %	10-11 (N=23) %	12 and over (N=24) %
Frequent/occasional symptoms	42	46	48	17
Symptom-free	58	54	52	83
Total	100	100	100	100

Chi-square = 9.46, 3 df, p < .02

Sex

At Time 1 girls were significantly more likely to be free of these neurotic symptoms than were boys, as Table 6-2 indicates.

Table 6-2

Neurotic Symptoms Score and Sex of Child

Score	Girls (N=61) %	Boys (N=64) %
Frequent symptoms	13	33
Occasional symptoms	33	28
Symptom-free	54	39
Total	100	100

Chi-square = 6.97, 2 df, p < .03

At Time 2, the same direction of difference is seen, but it misses statistical significance at the .05 level.

The boys, as we have seen, were significantly more aggressive than the girls, a difference that can be explained on grounds of general societal expectations, not peculiar to the problem of transracial adoption. The difference in symptomatology cannot be so explained. This may be further evidence that the combination of being male, black and adopted presents an unusually heavy emotional burden.

Number of Children in the Home

The more children living in the home at the time of initial interview, the greater the likelihood that the child would be free of the symptoms represented in the neurotic index score.

Table 6-3

Neurotic Symptoms Score and Number of Children in the Home

Score	1 or 2 Children (N=24) %	3 or 4 Children (N=69) %	5 or More Children (N=32) %
Frequent/occasional symptoms	71	55	38
Symptom-free	29	45	62
Total	100	100	100

Chi-square = 6.26, 2 df, p < .04

At the second interview, the relationship is in the same direction, but again the difference is not statistically significant.

Age of the Mother

Children whose mothers were 40 or over were significantly more likely to be free of symptoms than those whose mothers were younger.

Table 6-4

Neurotic Symptoms Score and Age of the Mother

Score	Under 40 (N=43) %	40 & Over (N=82) %
Frequent symptoms	35	17
Occasional symptoms	35	28
Symptom-free	30	55
Total	100	100

Chi-square = 7.98, 2 df, p < .02

One would expect the relationship between the age of the mother and the presence or absence of neurotic symptoms to be accounted for by the relationship of both with the age of the child. However, the mother's age accounts for a statistically significant portion of the variance (3%) in the symptoms score even when controlling for the age of the child. The same relationship between the neurotic symptom score and the age of the mother was seen in the analysis of the second-interview data, in which 64% of the mothers who were 40 or over had children who were symptom-free in contrast to 45% of those under 40.

Unmatched Expectations

The one variable specific to the adoption situation that influences the neurotic symptoms score is the failure of the child to match the intellectual preferences of the parents. The 27 children whose intelligence was either lower or higher than their parents had expected were more likely to have frequent symptoms than those who matched their parents' expectations or whose parents had no preference. The latter were more likely to have occasional symptoms or to be symptom-free.

Table 6-5

Neurotic Symptoms Score and Unmatched Expectations
on Intellectual Level

Score	No Preference/ Matched (N=98) %	Preference Not Matched (N=27) %
Frequent symptoms	18	41
Occasional symptoms	33	22
Symptom-free	49	37
Total	100	100

Chi-square = 5.98, 2 df, p < .06

Physical Symptoms Index

It could reasonably be argued that the cluster of related
physical symptoms--colds, headaches and tiredness--is not necessarily a valid outcome measure on grounds that most of the children
placed in adoption came from deprived backgrounds and may have been
more vulnerable to medical problems. It may also be argued that
the children in the youngest (and largest) age group in the study
were in the period in which children are particularly vulnerable
to respiratory infections they would outgrow as do other children.
In this analysis, however, the relationship with age is the reverse
of what would be expected from this reasoning. Furthermore, the
parents' perception of the child's blackness, a variable specific
to transracial adoption, is related to the incidence of physical
symptoms. The analysis suggests that some of the underlying problems in transracial adoption are reflected in the child's physical
symptoms, if one contrasts those children with the strongest symptoms to the rest of the sample.

Age and Physical Symptoms

The incidence of frequent physical symptoms increases directly with the age of the child. Children in the youngest age group are nearly all free of anything but occasional symptoms, whereas over a quarter of the children between 8 and 9 and two-fifths of those aged 10 and over have frequent symptoms.

Table 6-6

Physical Symptoms Score and Age of Child

Score	6-7 (N=48) %	8-9 (N=36) %	10 and over (N=41) %
Frequent symptoms	8	25	42
Occasional symptoms/ symptom-free	92	75	58
Total	100	100	100

Chi-square = 13.33, 2 df, p < .002

At the second interview, the same pattern is seen, and the relation is significant at the .05 level. Only 16% of the 6- and 7-year-olds have frequent symptoms, in contrast to 33% of the 8- and 9-year-olds and 46% of those 10 and over.

Perception of Blackness

Parents who said that their children are not obviously black were significantly more likely to report a pattern of frequent physical symptoms than those who perceived the child's blackness as obvious. This relationship, however, is not present at Time 2.

Table 6-7

Physical Symptoms Score and Perception of Blackness

Score	Obviously Black (N=62) %	Not Obviously Black (N=51) %
Frequent symptoms	13	33
Occasional symptoms	42	37
Symptom-free	45	29
Total	100	100

Chi-square = 7.26, 2 df, p < .03

Some of the ways in which the neurotic symptoms scores contrast to the physical symptoms scores may be noted. The incidence of neurotic symptoms declines with age, while the incidence of physical symptoms increases. Most of the variance on the neurotic symptoms score is accounted for by variables not specifically connected with adoption. In the case of physical symptoms, a variable specific to transracial adoption--the perception of blackness--has a significant effect.

Total Symptoms Score

The total symptoms score may also be seen as a measure of success on the grounds that the more symptoms of any kind reported in the child, the stronger the indication of some form of maladjustment, even though the nature of the total score is less specific than that of the physical or the neurotic symptoms scores. The total symptoms score may also reflect the extent to which parents are observant of or sensitive to the kinds of symptoms mentioned.

The more health-conscious parent may be more aware of symptoms, and the more anxious parent may report any given symptom as occurring "frequently" whereas the less anxious parent may report it as "occasional."

The analysis indicated that the total symptoms score was significantly related to four variables, one of which was demographic in nature and three of which were attitudinal. All account for statistically significant proportions of variance on the total symptoms score but none are interrelated, an indication that several different conditions influence the reporting of symptoms. None of the differences observed in the analysis of the first interview data persisted in the second interview.

Mother's Education

Supporting the suggestion that the total symptoms score may simply reflect the mother's awareness is the fact that the more educated mothers reported more symptoms.

Table 6-8

Total Symptoms Score and Mother's Education

Score	High School (N=32) %	College (N=93) %
Moderate/high	31	52
Minimal/low	69	48
Total	100	100

Chi-square = 3.97, 1 df, $p < .05$

Social Motivation

Parents who gave social reasons for adopting transracially--
such as a desire to make a home for a child who needed it[1]--
reported fewer symptoms in their children than those who did not.

Table 6-9

Total Symptoms Score and Reason For
Adopting Transracially

Score	"Social" (N=68) %	"Personal"/ "Second Choice" (N=57) %
Moderate/high	35	60
Minimal/low	65	40
Total	100	100

Chi-square = 6.45, 1 df, p < .01

Convictions About Transracial Adoption

Parents who entertained some doubts about the validity of
totally transracial adoption were likely to describe more symptoms
in their children, as well as to have children with higher inhibition scores.

---

1. This variable should not be confused with the reason for adoption. Parents were asked not only their reason for adoption
   but their reason for transracial adoption. Answers to the
   latter question could be categorized as "social," "personal
   motivation" or "second choice" (Table 3-2 in Chapter 3). Some
   parents whose original motivation for adoption was infertility
   gave social reasons for their interest in adopting transracially.
   Thus, this variable is not identical with the reason for adoption but is related to it.

Table 6-10

Total Symptoms Score and Convictions About
Totally Transracial Adoption

Score	Encouragement (N=56) %	Doubts (N=57) %
Moderate/high	39	54
Minimal/low	61	46
	—	—
Total	100	100

Chi-square = 2.59, 1 df, p < .10

This relationship misses statistical significance at the .05 level, but in the regression analysis the parents' convictions account for a significant proportion of the variance (4%) in the symptoms scores. We do not know whether a cause-effect relation is operating, or whether the apparent relation is due to another variable we did not identify.

Perception of Cruelty

As noted in Chapter 2, almost half the parents reported that their children had experienced some form of cruelty in their contacts with the community. When this variable was related to the outcome measures, no significant relationship appeared with any of the symptoms scores. Further analysis, however, indicated that the incidence of such experiences was related to the child's appearance; the darker children were exposed to more than the light ones, as would be expected (see Chapter 9). When we controlled for child's appearance, a significant relationship with the total symptoms score appears; but it is the reverse of what would be expected if the variable were an accurate description of the child's experience: children whose parents reported such experiences are more likely to be symptom-free than those whose parents denied, or did not know whether their children had had such experiences.

Table 6-11

Total Symptoms Score and the Parents' Perception of
Cruelty to Children of Dark Appearance

Score	Some Experience (N=40) %	Unknown/None (N=18) %
Moderate/high	27	61
Minimal/low	73	39
Total	100	100

Chi-square = 4.61, 1 df, p < .05

This phenomenon, in which positive rather than negative outcomes are associated with reporting of cruelty, is also seen in the findings reported in Chapter 8, and is discussed more fully later.

Summary

A pattern of relatively frequent neurotic symptoms (bed-wetting, nightmares, restlessness) was more common in children under 12, in boys, in children with mothers under 40, and in those in smaller families. The fact that the child did not match the parents' intellectual preferences was also associated with these symptoms. The relationships to the age of the child and to the age of the mother recur in the analysis of the data collected in the second interview, even though fewer symptoms were reported.

A pattern of relatively frequent physical symptoms (colds, headaches, tiredness) appeared more often in children over 10 years old. It was also seen more frequently in children described by their parents as not obviously black.

The total symptoms score derived from the first interview was higher for children whose mothers were educated at college level. High scores were also associated with adoption for reasons other than social motivation, and with doubts about the validity of totally transracial adoption. Low scores were associated with the parents' reports of experiences of cruelty.

Chapter 7

SUCCESS AS SEEN BY INTERVIEWERS, TEACHERS, AND PARENTS

One of the most common methods of evaluating the success of
any complex social action is to ask those who are concerned for
judgments on several aspects of the action and to combine their
responses into an overall judgment. Those making the judgments
usually vary in the extent to which they are involved with and
knowledgable about the subject of the evaluation. In this instance,
the evaluations obtained ranged from the presumably most objective
but least informed ratings made by the interviewer; to those of the
child's teacher, who is more involved and may be better informed
than the interviewer but less so than the parents; to the parents
themselves, whose investment in and knowledge of the child are
obviously the greatest. Each of these measures shows a different
pattern of relationships with the independent variables. This
chapter first considers two indices combining several different
ratings made by the interviewers, then the teachers' judgments,
and finally the parents' assessment of their experience.

Interviewer Ratings: Family Relationships

Ratings made by the interviewers after the first interview
were combined into an index reflecting their assessments of the
relationship of 1) the parents to each other, 2) the father to the
study child, 3) the mother to the study child, 4) the father to the
other children, and 5) the mother to the other children. Most of

these ratings were on the positive side, but there was a minority of families (28%) whom interviewers assessed as less warm than was usually the case. The analysis indicated that three variables were significantly related to positive or negative evaluations of the family's relationships: geographic location, the reason for the adoption, and mother's permissiveness.

Region

In contrast to all other respondents, a large majority of the Canadian families received low ratings. Families located in New England were also more likely than others to receive low ratings, but the difference is much less marked than for the Canadians.

Table 7-1

Interviewer Rating of Family Relations
and Geographic Location

Family Relations	Canada (N=19) %	New England (N=29) %	East North Central (N=17) %	West North Central (N=25) %	Pacific (N=35) %
Not warm	74	31	12	16	17
Warm/very warm	26	69	88	84	83
	—	—	—	—	—
Total	100	100	100	100	100

Chi-square = 25.86, 4 df, p < .001

Why these two locations were associated with negative interviewer ratings is difficult to explain. It is possible that cultural factors that result in undemonstrativeness or a greater reserve in the presence of outsiders were operating here.

Reason for Adoption

Interviewers tended to see in a more positive light the families who gave inability to have children as their reason for adopting than families who gave other reasons.

Table 7-2

Interviewer Rating and Reason for Adoption

Family Relations	Infertility (N=48) %	Social/Personal (N=77) %
Not warm	17	35
Warm	27	30
Very warm	56	35
Total	100	100

Chi-square = 6.73, 2 df, p < .03

Adoption for reasons of infertility is characteristic of the urbanites whom the interviewers generally tended to favor, as is shown in Chapter 10. The regression analysis indicated that the reason for adoption accounted by itself for a statistically significant degree of variance (3%) in the interviewer ratings. Since inability to have children biologically is the expected reason for seeking to adopt a child, it may well be that it is more acceptable to social worker/interviewers. It is also likely that social workers respond better to the frank acknowledgment of problems such as infertility than they do to other personal reasons or to claims of altruistic motives, about which they may be more skeptical.

Mother's Permissiveness

Although the measure of mother's permissiveness was derived from the questionnaire and permissiveness was not directly discussed in the interview, the analysis indicated a significant relationship between the mother's score on this measure and the interviewer ratings of the family's relationships. Mothers with a middle-range score, neither too permissive nor very strict, were most likely to be seen as having very warm relationships.

Table 7-3

Interviewer Rating and Mother's Permissiveness

Family Relations	Strict/ Permissive (N=78) %	Middle-range (N=46) %
Not warm	33	19
Warm	32	22
Very warm	35	59
	—	—
Total	100	100

Chi-square = 6.89, 2 df, p < .03

This relationship is not surprising, since such a balance between the extremes of permissiveness and strictness is generally considered the best parental approach to discipline. Extremes in either direction are more likely to be considered signs of disturbance and potentially damaging to the children. That such a "balanced" approach may also have unfavorable effects is suggested by the finding reported in Chapter 5 in which high aggression was associated with middle-range scores on permissiveness for the fathers.

Interviewer Ratings: Ability to Handle Racial Issues

After the second interview, the interviewers were asked to make another series of ratings, two of which referred to the relationship between the parents and the child, while four referred specifically to the racial aspects of the adoption. These ratings covered 1) the relationship of the mother to the child, 2) the relationship of the father to the child, 3) mother's ability to acknowledge the child's blackness, 4) father's ability to acknowledge the child's blackness, 5) the parents' feeling tone (degree of comfort) when responding to race-related questions, 6) the likelihood of problems for the child due to racial differences, 7) overall evaluation of how the adoption had worked out.

The analysis indicated that this rating of ability to handle racial issues, like the rating of family relationships made after the first interview, was related to the geographic location of the families. Four other variables were also associated with this rating.

Region

Families in Canada and New England were more likely to receive negative evaluations than families in any other location.

Table 7-4

Interviewer Rating on Racial Issues
and Geographic Location

Rating	Canada (N=17) %	New England (N=27) %	East North Central (N=15) %	West North Central (N=24) %	Pacific (N=31) %
Negative	65	52	13	21	19
Positive/very positive	35	48	87	79	81
	—	—	—	—	—
Total	100	100	100	100	100

Chi-square = 18.81, 4 df, p < .001

Mother's Education

A variable characteristic of the urban mother is the higher level of education, which accounts for 5% of the variance in the interviewer ratings of the handling of racial issues. The analysis indicated that the majority of mothers who had only a high school education received a low rating on this measure, while those with some college education tended to receive positive ratings, and college graduates usually received very positive ratings.

The explanations for this may be a mixture of reality and subjective reactions. College-educated mothers may well have been more knowledgable, sophisticated, and freer than others in discussing and handling racial matters. It is also possible that interviewers expected them to be able to handle racial matters better, and this too may have had an influence on the ratings given.

Table 7-5

Interviewer Rating on Racial Issues and Mother's Education

Rating	High School (N=28) %	Some College (N=33) %	College Graduate (N=53) %
Negative	61	27	23
Positive	11	46	22
Very positive	28	27	55
	—	—	—
Total	100	100	100

Chi-square = 21.82, 4 df, p < .001

Church Attendance

Mothers who attended church regularly were more likely to have positive ratings on their ability to handle racial issues than those who attended church irregularly or not at all.

Table 7-6

Interviewer Rating on Racial Issues and Church Attendance

Rating	Regular Church Attendance (N=74) %	Irregular/ None (N=40) %
Negative	26	48
Positive/very positive	74	52
	—	—
Total	100	100

Chi-square = 5.57, 1 df, p < .02

At the time of the first interview, the regular churchgoers drew a larger proportion of the highest (very warm) ratings (49%) than did the nonchurchgoers (32%), but there was only a 2% difference in the proportions assessed negatively.

Satisfaction With Agency Services

The extent to which the family expressed satisfaction with the service they received from their agency was related to the interviewer's ratings on racial issues. The relationship, however, was more complex than expected. Most parents who were satisfied with agency service received positive ratings by the interviewers on their ability to handle racial issues. Of those who expressed some dissatisfaction, it was the milder rather than the stronger expressions of dissatisfaction that were associated with negative ratings.

Table 7-7

Interviewer Rating on Racial Issues
and Satisfaction with Services

Rating	Dissatisfied (N=41) %	Somewhat Dissatisfied (N=37) %	Satisfied (N=35) %
Negative	29	51	17
Positive	32	22	26
Very positive	39	27	57
Total	100	100	100

Chi-square = 11.48, 4 df, p < .02

Mother's Openness to the Handicapped

The mother's openness to the adoption of the physically handicapped accounts for 6% of the variance in the interviewer ratings of the family's ability to handle the racial aspects of the adoption, more than any other single variable. As Table 7-8 indicates, the more open the mother was to the possibility of adopting a handicapped child, the more likely the interviewer was to give her a favorable rating on the handling of racial issues.

Table 7-8

Interviewer Rating on Racial Issues and Mother's
Openness to Adoption of the Handicapped

Rating	Not Open (N=32) %	Somewhat Open (N=34) %	Open (N=47) %
Negative	59	32	15
Positive	22	21	34
Very positive	19	47	51
Total	100	100	100

Chi-square = 18.58, 4 df, p < .001

These variables are independent of each other, since the rating was made a year after the data on openness were obtained and the latter information was in the mother's questionnaire, not the interview.

Interviewer Bias

These findings present a mixed bag of evidence on the validity of using trained interviewers' ratings as a measure of success. As can be seen later, interviewers favor urban families, which included more educated mothers, over small-town families. Yet by most other criteria, small-town families are as likely to have successful adoptions as urban families. Interviewers favor the mothers who strike a balance between permissiveness and strictness; yet there is no evidence by any other criterion used in the study that the mother's disciplinary style had anything to do with the success of the adoption. On the other hand, the reason for adopting, the degree of satisfaction with agency services, and the mother's openness to the adoption of a handicapped child are related not only to the interviewers' ratings but to several other criteria for successful outcome. Perhaps the best that can be said is that, although the judgments of trained social worker/interviewers may have some value, they should not be the sole measure of success.

Teacher Evaluations

If there is a measure of doubt about the interviewers' evaluations, what of the teachers'? These are adults who have more direct and extensive knowledge of the child than the interviewers and who are presumably more objective than the parents. On the other hand, the teachers' views are specialized and their judgments are relative to other children in their classes. The study children may be too new to them or may not stand out. The analysis is further limited by the fact that the teacher evaluation forms were returned for only 92 of the 125 children. Nevertheless, five independent variables were significantly related to the summary score based on teacher evaluations, when those children with the most negative assessments were compared with the rest of the sample. Unlike the interviewer assessments, all of these relationships apply to variables that are independent of the teachers' knowledge, and all are related to other outcome criteria as well.

Sex

The child's sex accounts for more variance in teachers' evaluations than any other variable (7%). Boys are much more likely than girls to be evaluated unfavorably by their teachers.

Table 7-9

Teacher Rating and Sex of Child

Teacher Rating	Girls (N=44) %	Boys (N=48) %
Low	21	44
Average/high	79	56
Total	100	100

Chi-square = 4.66, 1 df, p < .03

This pattern is consistent with the higher aggression scores made by the boys on the Missouri Children's Behavior Checklist and their higher scores on the neurotic symptoms index, which includes restlessness. However, it should be noted that there were no sex differences on the California Test of Personality, on the indices measuring peer and sibling relations, and on the measures dealing specifically with the racial aspects of the adoption.

Length of Time in Placement

Time in placement is also a factor in the teacher evaluation, but only when one compares the relatively small group of children (15) who have been in their adoptive homes for less than 5 years with the rest of the sample. More than half of this group have low ratings, in contrast to slightly more than a quarter of the rest of the sample.

Table 7-10

Teacher Rating and Time in Placement

Teacher Rating	3-4 Years (N=15) %	5 or More Years (N=77) %
Low	60	27
Average/high	40	73
	---	---
Total	100	100

Chi-square = 4.72, 1 df, p < .03

This is consistent with the finding reported earlier that children in placement for the shortest time had the lowest social adjustment scores. This finding also supports the inference that a period of almost 5 years is needed before most of the children and their families are able to achieve a fully satisfactory adjustment.

Years of Marriage

Another variable related to the teacher rating is the length of the parents' marriage at the time of placement. There is no

evidence that this is a spurious relationship resulting from a
link with another variable such as the age of the parents. Yet
the nature of the relationship makes it suspect. It is bimodal
in that both the parents married a relatively short time (under
10 years) and those married longest (15 years or more) have a disproportionate number of children given low ratings by their teachers.
By contrast, nearly all children of parents who had been married
10 to 14 years have average or high ratings. The low teacher
ratings for children of parents married less than 10 years are
consistent with the finding of high aggression scores for these
children. The shift in pattern for children of marriages that
have lasted 15 years or more as compared with those of 10 to 14
years' duration lends itself to no ready explanation.

Table 7-11

Teacher Rating and Years of Parents' Marriage

Teacher Rating	Under 10 Years (N=40) %	10-14 Years (N=30) %	15 or More Years (N=22) %
Low	42	13	41
Average/high	58	87	59
	—	—	—
Total	100	100	100

Chi-square = 7.54, 2 df, p < .05

Intellectual Preference

Parents who said they preferred a child of average intelligence
were twice as likely to have a child who had a low teacher rating

than those who had initially preferred high intelligence or who had no preference.

Table 7-12

Teacher Rating and Parents'
Intellectual Preference

Teacher Rating	Preferred Average (N=23) %	All Others (N=69) %
Low	52	26
Average/high	48	74
	---	---
Total	100	100

Chi-square = 4.22, 1 df, p < .04

Since many of the parents who preferred children of average intelligence received children of a higher level of ability than they expected, this relationship is not explained by the actual ability of the child. It is possible that a preference for a child with average intelligence is related to lack of concern for school achievement, so that the children of these parents are not at their best in school.

Parents' Satisfaction[1]

The adoptive parents are, of course, at one and the same time the adults most knowledgable about the study child and also the most

1. All the findings are based on the Time 1 measure of parental satisfaction. The score for the Time 2 measure was incorporated in the summary index, but the analysis of the Time 2 index of family satisfaction in relation to the independent variables was not productive and is not presented here.

heavily invested in the success of the adoption. Most parental assessments of the success of the adoption were, as expected, positive, but when a series of somewhat different assessments are combined into a single index, one can distinguish a range of attitudes from the totally satisfied, to the generally satisfied, and to those with some doubts or misgivings about the success of their venture into adoption.

This index was made up of the responses to eight questions: 1) the mother's statement about the ease of rearing the study child, 2) the equivalent statement from the father, 3) the parents' assessment of the child's school performance, 4) the mother's statement about the degree of satisfaction she had derived from the experience with the study child, 5) the equivalent statement from the father, 6) the mother's statement that adoption enabled her to express deep love, 7) the mother's statement about the effect of the adoption on the marriage, 8) the equivalent statement from the father.

The degree of parental satisfaction was shown to vary significantly with the extent to which the family has contact with its relatives, and with the racial composition of the neighborhood. It also varied with two attitudinal variables: the mother's openness to the adoption of the handicapped, and both parents' satisfaction with their relationship with the adoption agency.

Contact With Relatives

The more contact the parents had with their relatives, the stronger the expression of satisfaction with the adoption.

-165-

Table 7-13

Satisfaction of Parents and Contact With Relatives

Satisfaction	Less Than Once a Month (N=61) %	1-3 Contacts a Month (N=30) %	Once a Week or More (N=34) %
Low	43	27	23
Average	31	46	24
High	26	27	53
	—	—	—
Total	100	100	100

Chi-square = 10.84, 4 df, p < .03

This relationship suggests several explanations. Parents who have good relationships with their extended families may also be those best able to absorb an adopted child of a different race; they anticipate support from their families and are encouraged to adopt. The supportiveness of the extended family in turn reinforces their satisfaction with the adoption. On the other hand, some parents have reduced contact with some members of their families because of the adoption, and the lack of contact in turn may limit the satisfaction they derive from the adoption.

Racial Composition of Neighborhood

Parents living in neighborhoods that are not totally white were almost twice as likely as the families in white neighborhoods to report a high degree of satisfaction with their experience in adopting the study child.

Table 7-14

Satisfaction of Parents and Race of Neighborhood

Satisfaction	Totally White (N=56) %	Not Totally White (N=69) %
Low	45	25
Average	32	33
High	23	42
Total	100	100

Chi-square = 6.95, 2 df, p < .03

This finding is not surprising or difficult to explain. Living in neighborhoods that are not totally white may mean more black friends, more resources for dealing with cultural matters, and lower visibility for the child, all of which may combine to reduce the problems and tensions inherent in transracial adoption. It should be noted that the description of the neighborhood was not based on any objective criterion, but depended on the parents' observations. It is possible that the neighborhoods were less mixed or more mixed than the parents perceived. Those in the "not totally white" neighborhoods may be the parents who are more sensitized to the racial aspects of the adoption than others, more aware of homes where nonwhites live, and more likely to seek them out. It is also worth noting that this variable affects only the parents' satisfaction with the adoption and is not related to any of the measures that reflect the child's adjustment more directly.

Mother's Openness to the Adoption of the Handicapped

The more open the mother is to the adoption of handicapped children, the more likely she is to express satisfaction with the study child's adoption.

Table 7-15

Satisfaction of Parents and Mother's Openness
to the Adoption of the Handicapped

Satisfaction	Not Open/ Ambivalent (N=72) %	Open (N=53) %
Low	42	23
Average	32	34
High	26	43
Total	100	100

Chi-square = 5.96, 2 df, p < .06

This too is a relationship that can be interpreted in either direction. A mother's positive responses to the questions about adopting other types of hard-to-place children may reflect a more general maternal drive and openness to the experience of mothering. The underlying maternal drive would then be associated with greater satisfaction in the adoption, which this measure was intended to reflect. On the other hand, it is also possible that satisfaction with this adoption made some mothers more open to another type of adoption experience.

Satisfaction With Agency Service

Parental satisfaction with the adoption varies directly with the degree of satisfaction felt by the parents with the agency's handling of the adoption process.

Again, this is a plausible relationship, but it too can be interpreted in either direction. It is certainly likely that parents who were satisfied with the agency's handling of the adoption would also express satisfaction with the adoption experience as a whole. It is also possible that parents whose experience with their adopted child had been less than satisfying are retrospectively dissatisfied with the agency, feeling that it might have done a better job either in the selection of the child or in the preparation they were given for the adoption.

Table 7-16

Satisfaction of Parents and Satisfaction With Agency

Satisfaction	Dissatisfied (N=41) %	Some Dissatisfaction (N=40) %	Satisfied (N=44) %
Low	39	42	21
Average	41	28	29
High	20	30	50
Total	100	100	100

Chi-square = 11.09, 4 df, p < .03

Summary

Ratings by interested or knowledgable adults of the success of the transracial adoptions show varying influences. Interviewer ratings of the quality of family relationships tended to be unfavorable for families living in Canada and New England, and for families giving reasons for adopting other than infertility. They were more favorable for mothers who show a balance between permissiveness and strictness in their child-rearing practices. Interviewer ratings of parental ability to handle the racial aspects of adoption also tended to be unfavorable for families in Canada and New England. They favored mothers who were educated beyond the high school level and were regular churchgoers. They favored those who were open to the idea of adopting handicapped children and those who were satisfied with agency services.

Teachers tended to give higher ratings to girls than to boys. Children in placement more than 5 years tended to have higher teacher ratings than those in placement a shorter time, as did children whose parents had been married 10 to 14 years, as compared with all other children. Parents who had expressed a preference for a child of average intelligence were more likely to have children with low teacher ratings.

Parental satisfaction with the adoption tended to be high when parents had frequent contact with relatives, when they lived in neighborhoods that were not totally white, when the mother was open to the idea of adopting a handicapped child, and when the parents were satisfied with their experience with the adoption agency.

Chapter 8

PEER RELATIONS AS A MEASURE OF SUCCESS

Most, if not all, transracially adopted children eventually
face the problem of high visibility among their peers. The child
may be the only black child in a family of several white children,
the only one or among a few on the block, in the neighborhood, or
in the school system. Good relationships with siblings and with
other children are normally an indication of any child's successful
adjustment, and they are, if anything, even more significant as an
indication of successful adjustment for children adopted across
racial lines.

As the data in Chapter 2 indicated, most study children did
well in both respects. Originally it was expected that good relations with siblings and with other children would be part of the
parents' overall evaluation of the adoption, but the analysis indicated that the items used as measures of these aspects of the
child's adjustment were not necessarily correlated with the items
in the parents' evaluations; that is, parents who reported difficulties in these areas were not necessarily unhappy with the adoption,
and vice versa. Furthermore, the parents' statements on relationships
with siblings were not strongly associated with their statements of
relationships with other children. These two aspects of peer relations were therefore analyzed separately and each produced a different pattern of relationships with the independent variables examined.

Relations With Siblings

The index of sibling relations was composed of three statements made by the parents about 1) the study child's ability to get along with his siblings, 2) his feelings about the siblings, 3) the siblings' feelings about him.

When the children having low scores on sibling relations are compared with the others, they differ significantly on three variables: the number of children in the family, the family's social life, and the mother's attitude toward blacks.

Number of Siblings

Study children who entered a family with two children were much more likely than children in any other kind of family constellation to have problematic relations with siblings.

Table 8-1

Relations With Siblings and
Number of Children at Placement*

Relationship	Two Siblings (N=28) %	All Others (N=92) %
Problematic	43	16
Good	32	45
Very good	25	39
Total	100	100

Chi-square = 8.72, 2 df, p < .01

*As five children had no siblings, N=120.

Social Life

Families who saw their friends no more than once a month described poor sibling relations less often than did families who reported seeing their friends two to three times a month or oftener.

The sibling relations index is the only outcome measure that is associated with measures of the parents' social life. It is possible that in the more isolated families the siblings are forced to rely on each other as playmates to a greater extent than in the families with a more normal pattern of social activity. It is also possible that the more isolated parents want to feel that their children get along well and therefore do not need other contacts.

Table 8-2

Relations With Siblings and
Extent of Family's Social Life

Relationship	Once a Month or Less (N=39) %	More Than Once a Month (N=81) %
Problematic	8	31
Good	54	35
Very good	38	34
	—	—
Total	100	100

Chi-square = 7.80, 2 df, p < .02

Mother's Attitudes Toward Blacks

The mothers who took somewhat conservative views on blacks (see Table 2-15) were less likely than the more liberal majority to report problematic relations with siblings.

-173-

Table 8-3

Sibling Relations and Mother's
Attitude Toward Blacks

Relationship	Uncertain/ Conservative (N=32) %	Problack (N=77) %
Problematic	6	31
Good	50	38
Very good	44	31
	——	——
Total	100	100

Chi-square = 7.74, 2 df, p < .02

When the index reflecting the father's attitude on blacks and the one reflecting both parents' positions were cross-tabulated against this form of outcome, the pattern was the same but not so strong.

Since this measure of the mother's attitude toward blacks was not related to any of the other variables found to be associated with sibling relationships, we have no evidence that this finding is spurious; it may, however, be more the result of chance than anything else.

Relations With Other Children

The index measuring the extent to which the study child got along with children other than siblings was composed of four statements made by the parents describing 1) the study child's general ability to get along with children, 2) his ability to get along with younger children, 3) his ability to get along with older children, 4) the parents' assessment of his popularity.

When the children whose relations with others were considered problematic were compared with the rest of the sample, the analysis showed significant relationships with the father's employment, his openness to the adoption of a handicapped child, and the parents' perception of the extent to which the study children had been exposed to cruelty by other children.

Father's Occupation

Fathers who had a professional occupation were less likely than other fathers to report problems in the ability of the study child to get along with other children.

It should be noted that the father's occupation bears no such relation to the quality of sibling relations. It may be that the standing of professionals in the neighborhood or the community leads to a greater prestige for and acceptance of their children by others.

Table 8-4

Relations With Children and Father's Occupation

Relationship	Professional (N=64) %	All Others (N=51) %
Problematic	8	26
Good	47	47
Very good	45	27
	—	—
Total	100	100

Chi-square = 6.62, 2 df, p < .03

Father's Openness to the Adoption of a Handicapped Child

Fathers with a middle-range score on this index were more likely to report that the study child had problems in relating to other children than those who were either definitely open or not open on this point.

Table 8-5

Relations With Children and Father's Openness to the Adoption of the Handicapped

Relationship	Not Open (N=43) %	Somewhat Open (N=41) %	Open (N=30) %
Problematic	5	24	13
Good	65	29	47
Very good	30	46	40
Total	100	100	100

Chi-square = 12.97, 4 df, p < .01

As in the case of permissiveness-strictness, middle-range scores on this item suggest ambivalence or inconsistency on the part of the father. It is not difficult to see that problems in the study child's relations with other children might be associated with such parental attitudes. What is more puzzling is why this is reflected in the father's attitude and not in the mother's, which shows no such association with the study child's problems in relating to other children. The mother's openness seems to be more related to the more global measures of success than the father's.

Parents' Perception of Cruelty

In the second interview, parents were asked whether the study child had been subjected to any form of cruelty by other children. As noted in Chapter 3, nearly half reported incidents usually involving name calling or "heckling." One-third of the parents denied that their children had experienced any kind of cruelty from other children, and the remainder said that the child's racial background was not known to his friends. Paradoxically, the children whose parents reported that they had experienced cruelty also reported significantly fewer, not more, problems in relationships with other children.

Table 8-6

Relations With Children and
Parents' Perception of Cruelty

Relationship	Some Cruelty Reported (N=56) %	No Cruelty Reported (N=58) %
Problematic	6	27
Good	46	40
Very good	48	33
	—	—
Total	100	100

Chi-square = 10.44, 2 df, p < .01

As was noted earlier, the analysis indicated that the parents' perception of cruelty is related to a strong problack position on the measure of attitudes toward blacks and to a high level of activity designed to introduce the child to his black heritage.

The more awareness of race on the part of both parents or the mother in particular, the more likely the parents were to report that the study child had experienced cruelty from other children. The reporting of cruelty was also associated, as would be expected, with the child's appearance; the darker children were more vulnerable than the lighter children. The analysis indicated, however, that the relationship between the absence of problems with other children and the reporting of cruelty holds for the darker children when controlling for the child's appearance, as Table 8-7 indicates.

Table 8-7

Relationships With Children and Parents' Perception of
Cruelty in Children of Relatively Light and Dark Appearance

| Relationship | Relatively Dark | | Relatively Light | |
	Cruelty Reported (N=40) %	No Cruelty Reported (N=18) %	Cruelty Reported (N=16) %	No Cruelty Reported (N=40) %
Problematic	3	33	13	25
Good/very good	97	67	87	75
Total	100	100	100	100

Chi-square = 8.40, 1 df, p < .01   Chi-square = 0.44, 1df, N.S.

On the surface, it seems paradoxical that the parents who were most prepared to deal with race problems had children who were most likely to experience them directly. On reflection, though, it seems more likely that the parents' awareness simply made them more conscious of such episodes and less likely to deal with them by denial. It is also likely that if racial matters were openly discussed in the household, the study children or their siblings were freer to report and discuss such incidents.

It is also possible that some form of defensive denial is playing a role here, similar to that discussed in the preceding section. Parents whose children have experienced episodes of cruelty may feel compelled to point out that, despite everything, the study child's relationships with other children are good. The significance of this variable along with others related to race is discussed in more detail in the next chapter.

Summary

Transracially adopted children entering families who already have two children tend to have more problematic sibling relations than do the study children entering other family constellations. Children in families who are relatively isolated socially are reported to have fewer problems in sibling relations than those who are more active, as are the children of mothers who are relatively conservative in their attitudes toward blacks.

Fathers in nonprofessional occupations were more likely to report problems in the study child's ability to relate to children generally than were fathers in the professions. Fathers who had mixed feelings about the possibility of adopting a handicapped child also reported problematic relations with other children more frequently than others. Finally, parents who reported that the study child had experienced some form of cruelty from other children were nevertheless more likely to report that the child had good relationships with other children than parents who denied or were unaware of such experience.

Chapter 9

ATTITUDES TOWARD BLACKNESS AS A MEASURE OF SUCCESS

All of the outcome measures discussed in the preceding chapters
could be considered valid measures of success or failure in any
adoption study, and most of them could also apply to studies of
the adjustment of any group of children who can be evaluated on
the basis of test scores, symptom lists, teachers' ratings, and
the observations of their parents. Black children in white homes,
however, have to come to terms with their heritage, as do all black
children, but living with white families is frequently presumed to
be an obstacle to such a goal and constitutes a major reason for
opposition to such adoptions. The extent to which the study
families were able to inculcate positive attitudes toward blackness in their adopted children thus becomes a measure of successful
outcome.

Parent responses to questions dealing with attitudes toward
blackness were described in Chapter 3. In most instances, from a
quarter to a third of the children were reported as having some
sort of negative feeling about being black. It must be borne in
mind, however, that for children in the age range covered by the
study, identity is in the prosess of formation, so that any expressed
feeling about blackness, positive or negative, may be transient.
Whether negative feelings are more common among the transracial

adoptees than among black children of comparable age reared in black families could be determined only by study of an appropriate comparison group of black children in black families.

Even with these limitations in mind, it is still instructive to examine some of the ways in which positive attitutdes on the part of the study children vary within the sample. The parents' responses to two of the questions asked in the area of racial atti-tudes were related to the independent variables used in the analysis. The first of these was the parents' response to the question asked during the first interview on whether the child suffered any dis-comfort about being different in appearance from the rest of the family. The second was the response to a request to the parents in the second interview to describe the child's attitude toward his black or part-black heritage. Factors associated with each of these responses are discussed in this chapter, as are factors related to the child's experience of cruelty. It is worth noting that these two forms of outcome, as the correlation matrix in Chapter 4 indicates, are unrelated to almost every other form of outcome. It is possible, then, for a study child to give evidence of problems in the area of black identity without showing signs of disturbance in other areas, and it is equally possible for the reverse pattern to be seen.

Discomfort About Appearance

A large majority (68%) of the parents denied that their chil-dren showed any discomfort about their differences in appearance from the rest of the family, but the remaining 32% reported that the study child did feel uncomfortable. Acknowledgment of such discomfort varied with the child's appearance; discomfort was reported much more frequently for the darker children, as would be expected.

Table 9-1

Discomfort About Appearance and Child's Appearance

Discomfort	Fair, No Negroid Features (N=20) %	Fair, Negroid Features/ Light Brown, No Negroid Features (N=41) %	Light Brown or Dark, Negroid Features (N=64) %
Yes	10	27	42
No	90	73	58
	—	—	—
Total	100	100	100

Chi-square = 8.01, 2 df, p < .02

However, the analysis also indicated that acknowledgment of such discomfort varied with parental awareness of race. An index called "Orientation to Race" was developed, which included six statements from the joint interview with the parents and from the individual interviews with each: 1) their concern about the difficulties the study child might face in relation to race, 2) whether they subscribed to black magazines, 3) whether they attended exhibits or other events concerning black culture, 4) whether they belonged to an organization of parents adopting transracially, 5) mother's statement that friends had discussed the possibility of transracial adoption with her, 6) the equivalent statement from

the father. The analysis indicated that parents who had high
scores on this measure, reflecting a high degree of awareness of
the racial aspects of the adoption, were much more likely to
report that their children were somewhat uncomfortable about their
appearance than were the parents with less awareness. Similarly,
parents who tended to be "problack" on the measure of attitudes
toward blacks derived from the questionnaire used at the time of
the second interview, were more likely to report such discomfort
than the more conservative parents.

Table 9-2

Discomfort About Appearance and Parents' Orientation
to Race (Time 1) and Attitudes Toward Blacks (Time 2)

Discomfort	Orientation to Race Time 1			Attitudes Toward Blacks Time 2	
	Low (N=42) %	Average (N=41) %	High (N=42) %	Uncertain (N=40) %	"Problack" (N=73) %
Yes	21	27	48	20	41
No	79	73	52	80	59
Total	100	100	100	100	100

Chi-square = 7.37, 2 df, p < .03   Chi-square = 4.25, 2 df, p < .05

When the child's appearance was held constant and the parents'
orientation toward race examined in relation to the child's reported
discomfort, it was found that parents with a strong problack orientation reported discomfort in relatively light children as well as
in those who were darker, while parents with a low score on this
measure reported discomfort only for the darkest children.

Parents' reports of the child's discomfort about his appearance apparently depend both on the child's actual appearance and on the perceptions of parents, some of whom are more conscious of the racial aspects of the adoption than others. The regression analysis indicated that two other variables accounted for more variance on the reports of discomfort than did either the child's appearance or the parents' orientation toward race, even when the latter variables are entered into the equation. One was the extent to which parents had reservations about adoption to begin with and the other was the mother's age.

Reservations About Transracial Adoption

As indicated in Chapter 3, parents were asked whether they had reservations about various aspects of transracial adoption when they first considered it. The responses to four of the questions asked were sufficiently intercorrelated to constitute an index called "Reservations About Adoption." This included the parents' reservations about 1) how a child of a different race would fit into their families, 2) what the neighbors might think, 3) how the neighborhood children would treat a child of a different race, 4) whether the child would be happy with parents of another race. Parents with low scores on this index had many reservations about what they were doing; those with high scores considered themselves relatively free of such anxieties. As one might expect, those with the most reservations reported that their children were uncomfortable about their appearance more than twice as frequently as those who were relatively free of reservations.

Table 9-3

Discomfort About Appearance and Reservations About Adoption

Discomfort	Some Anxiety (N=41) %	Slight Anxiety (N=34) %	No Anxiety (N=50) %
Yes	54	24	20
No	46	76	80
	—	—	—
Total	100	100	100

Chi-square = 13.27, 2 df, p < .01

This relationship holds, even with control for the parents' orientation to race. Whether they have low or high scores on this measure, the more anxious parents report more discomfort in their children.

Table 9-4

Discomfort About Appearance and Reservations
of Parents With Low and High Race Orientation Scores

Discomfort	High Race Orientation			Low Race Orientation	
	Some (N=29) %	Slight (N=22) %	None (N=32) %	Some (N=12) %	Slight/None (N=30) %
Yes	55	36	22	50	10
No	45	64	78	50	90
	—	—	—	—	—
Total	100	100	100	100	100

Chi-square = 7.22, 2 df,   Chi-square = 5.94, 1 df,
           p < .03   p < .02

Age of Mother

The younger the mother, the more likely she was to report that the child had some discomfort about his appearance.

-186-

Table 9-5

Discomfort About Appearance and Age of Mother

Discomfort	Under 40 (N=43) %	40-44 (N=43) %	45 and Over (N=39) %
Yes	44	37	13
No	56	63	87
	---	---	---
Total	100	100	100

Chi-square = 10.06, 2 df, $p < .01$

When the family's orientation to race is held constant, one finds that, among the mothers with high racial orientation, the younger mothers are still significantly more likely to report that the child has felt some discomfort about the difference between his appearance and that of the rest of the family.

Table 9-6

Discomfort About Appearance and Age of Mother
With High and Low Race Orientation Scores

Discomfort	High Race Orientation			Low Race Orientation		
	Under 40 (N=26) %	40-44 (N=28) %	45 and Over (N=29) %	Under 40 (N=17) %	40-44 (N=15) %	45 and Over (N=10) %
Yes	62	36	17	18	40	--
No	38	64	83	82	60	100
	---	---	---	---	---	---
Total	100	100	100	100	100	100

Chi-square = 11.54, 2 df, $p < .02$ Chi-square = 5.94, 2 df, $p < .06$

The age of the father shows the same pattern, but it is not so strong as the mother's age. One might infer that younger parents have younger or more recently placed children who are still not entirely at home with the family, but no such relationship between the age of the child or the time in placement is seen when these variables are cross-tabulated against the discomfort reported. The inference, then, is that younger parents are more sensitive on this point than are the older ones, regardless of the age of the child.

Attitude Toward Black Heritage

When they were interviewed for a second time, parents were asked to describe the child's attitude toward his black heritage. One-third of the children were described as proud of it. For a larger group (44%), the parents said either that they did not know the child's attitude or that he appeared indifferent. Twenty-four percent of the children were described as having attitudes with negative connotations: confusion, embarrassment or anger. Whether the child's attitude was positive varied with two demographic variables: the father's occupation and the child's age at placement. Such attitudes also varied with one aspect of the family's life style--the frequency of contact with relatives--and, as would be expected, with the parents' attitudes toward blacks.

Father's Occupation

Study children in homes where the father is a professional were more likely than others to have a positive attitude toward their black heritage.

Table 9-7

Attitude Toward Black Heritage and
Father's Occupation

Attitude	Professional (N=60) %	All Others (N=45) %
Negative	20	24
Indifferent	37	55
Positive	43	21
	___	___
Total	100	100

Chi-square = 6.48, 2 df, p < .05

This relationship is in the expected direction. Since encouraging a positive attitude involves education, it is not surprising that fathers in the professions do better than others. However, when education is cross-tabulated with the child's reported attitude toward his black heritage, it is only the children of fathers with postgraduate degrees who show more positive attitudes, and the difference is not so strong as it is in the case of the father's occupation. The implication is that not only is education needed to encourage positive attitudes, but also required is the degree of commitment that generally accompanies entry into the service professions, which characterized most of the fathers in the professions.

Child's Age at Placement

Age at placement also appears to play a role in the attitude toward black heritage, but the nature of the relationship is unexpected. More of the children placed between 6 and 11 months of age are described as having negative or indifferent attitudes and less as having positive attitudes than any other group of children.

Table 9-8

Attitude Toward Black Heritage and Age at Placement

Attitude	6-11 Months (N=21) %	All Others (N=93) %
Negative	38	20
Indifferent	52	42
Positive	10	38
	——	——
Total	100	100

Chi-square = 6.85, 2 df, p < .05

The only clue as to why this age group of children should be more inclined to indifference or negativism on race is that, as Table 9-9 indicates, they were more likely than any other age group to be relatively light in appearance. Otherwise, the relationship between age at placement and appearance is expected; the darker children were much more likely than the lighter ones to be placed for adoption after their first birthday.

Table 9-9

Child's Appearance and Age at Placement

Appearance	Under 6 Months (N=30) %	6-11 Months (N=24) %	12-35 Months (N=51) %	36 Months and Over (N=20) %
Fair or light brown, no Negroid features	43	62	25	30
Fair to dark, Negroid features	57	38	75	70
	——	——	——	——
Total	100	100	100	100

Chi-square = 10.44, 3 df, p < .02

One may speculate that children in the 6-11 month age group were those for whom adoption may have been delayed until their skin coloring and the presence or absence of Negroid features was established and who were then placed with parents to whom a white appearance was important. Darker infants placed at birth may well have been placed with families to whom skin color was unimportant. However, the regression analysis, in which both the child's appearance and the age at placement were entered, indicated that the age of placement is the more influential variable, which is somewhat surprising and not easily explained.

Contact With Relatives

Families in frequent contact with relatives are much more likely than others to have children with positive attitudes toward their heritage. Conversely, the families most isolated from their relatives report the highest proportion of children who have negative feelings about black heritage.

Table 9-10

Attitude Toward Black Heritage and Contact With Relatives

Attitude	Less Than Once a Month (N=55) %	1-3 Times a Month (N=29) %	Once a Week or More (N=30) %
Negative	31	21	14
Indifferent	44	55	33
Positive	25	24	53
	---	---	---
Total	100	100	100

Chi-square = 9.76, 4 df, p < .05

Frequency of contact with relatives was related to the parents' satisfaction with the adoption, as noted in Chapter 7. It is a little more surprising that contact with relatives should be related to the child's attitude toward his heritage. It may be that the extended family's acceptance of the child makes it easier for him to see his black heritage in a positive light. Conversely, those children with adoptive grandparents, uncles, aunts, and so forth, who keep their distance because they disapprove of the adoption may still sense that something is wrong even when parents do their best to protect the children against such attitudes.

Orientation Toward Race

Not surprisingly, parents with the strongest racial orientation reported the highest proportion of children with a positive attitude toward their heritage.

Table 9-11

Attitude Toward Heritage and Parents'
Orientation to Race

Attitude	Low (N=39) %	Average (N=38) %	High (N=37) %
Negative	20	24	27
Indifferent	54	52	24
Positive	26	24	49
Total	100	100	100

Chi-square = 9.56, 4 df, p < .05

It is noteworthy that more of the most "aware" families produce
a positive attitude in their children, rather than an attitude of
indifference. The proportion of children described as having
negative attitudes is about the same for these families as for the
others.

The Perception of Cruelty

An obviously sensitive aspect of the transracially adopted
child's experience is the possibility of his exposure to social
cruelty. It is difficult, however, to determine whether exposure
to social cruelty should be treated as an independent variable
(cause) or a dependent variable (effect). Exposure to cruelty is
certainly an undesirable outcome from which these children need as
much protection as possible. On the other hand, adoptive parents
do not control community reactions any more than do black parents,
and they must do what black parents do: prepare their children
for and help them deal with these episodes when they happen. One
could then treat the experience of cruelty as an independent variable.

The speed of computer methods of data processing permitted us
to treat this variable both as independent and dependent, and relate
it to both the outcome and the independent variables used in the
study. Unfortunately, this did not solve all of the analytic problems inherent in this variable. As noted in the preceding chapters,
the response to this question was highly colored by the attitude of
the parents toward blacks. The more aware parents were of the

problems of being black, the more likely they were to report that their children had had experience of cruelty.

Analysis of the problem was also complicated by the fact that at least 17% of the study children were light enough to "pass" and still others were not conspicuous in their communities. Thus the possibility of exposure to such experiences was lower for some children than for others. Therefore, an analysis was done in which the white-appearing children were omitted from consideration. Even with this additional work, the findings on this variable have to be regarded as more tentative than others. They are presented because of the importance of their content.

Even when this variable is controlled for appearance, it is related only to two of the outcome variables discussed earlier: the total symptoms score and the child's relations with his peers. When one looks at it in relation to other independent variables, one finds that four are significant: the child's appearance, his sex, the size of the nonwhite population in the community, and the number of adopted children in the family.

Child's Appearance

As would be expected, such experiences are reported much more frequently for the darkest children than for the others. Parents also seemed much more certain as to whether or not the child had had such experiences in the case of the darkest children than they were for the lighter ones.

Table 9-12

Perception of Cruelty and Child's Appearance

Perception of Cruelty	Fair, No Negroid Features (N=19) %	Fair, Negroid Features/ Light Brown, No Negroid Features (N=37) %	Light Brown or Dark, Negroid Features (N=58) %
Cruelty reported	0	43	69
Uncertain/ unknown	63	22	2
No cruelty	37	35	29
	—	—	—
Total	100	100	100

Chi-square = 44.24, 4 df, p < .001

Sex of Child

More experiences of cruelty are reported for girls than for boys, but there is also more uncertainty as to what the boys have experienced. The proportion of boys and girls whose parents were certain they had not experienced any cruelty was about the same.

Table 9-13

Perception of Cruelty and Sex of the Child

Perception of Cruelty	Girls (N=55) %	Boys (N=59) %
Cruelty reported	62	37
Uncertain/unknown	7	29
No cruelty	31	34
	—	—
Total	100	100

Chi-square = 10.74, 2 df, p < .05

An analysis involving those children with clearly Negroid features indicated the same pattern; cruelty is reported more often for girls of dark appearance than for boys of dark appearance, but the difference is not statistically significant.

It is likely that girls may be freer to report unpleasant experiences than boys and may be more protected by siblings who will report such incidents to their parents. Boys may be more embarrassed to do so or not want their parents to know about any fights that may have resulted. Parents may sense this; hence the disproportionate number of "unknowns" in the case of boys.

Nonwhite Population

Episodes of cruelty were much less frequently reported by the small group of parents who live in communities where the population was more than 5% nonwhite.

Table 9-14

Perception of Cruelty and Nonwhite Population

Perception of Cruelty	Less Than 5% (N=85) %	More Than 5% (N=29) %
Cruelty reported	56	27
Uncertain/unknown	18	21
No cruelty	26	52
Total	100	100

Chi-square = 8.23, 2 df, p < .02

The analysis in which only the darker children were considered showed that the relationship still held at a statistically significant level.

-196-

When the perception of cruelty is cross-tabulated with the racial composition of the neighborhood, the pattern is similar. Fifty-nine percent of the parents in totally white neighborhoods report some experiences of cruelty, in contrast to 42% of those whose neighborhood is not totally white, but this difference is not statistically significant. This may imply that the racial composition of the total community has a stronger effect than that of the immediate neighborhood.

Number of Adoptions

In the original analysis, no relationship appeared between the number of adopted children in the family and reports of cruelty. However, the analysis involving only the darker children indicated that families having adopted three or more children reported more incidents of cruelty than did families with one or two adoptions.

Table 9-15

Experience of Cruelty in Children of Dark and Light Appearance and Number of Adopted Children in Family

Perception of Cruelty	Dark Appearance		Light Appearance	
	1-2 Adoptions (N=44) %	3 or More Adoptions (N=14) %	1-2 Adoptions (N=26) %	3 or More Adoptions (N=30) %
Cruelty reported	64	93	23	33
Unknown/none	36	7	77	67
Total	100	100	100	100

Chi-square = 3.56, 1 df, $p < .06$ Chi-square = 0.30, 1 df, N.S.

This relationship with respect to the darker children is not difficult to understand, since the families with more adoptees may have more non-Caucasian children and may be more sensitized to the cruelty problem than others. The racial mixture of larger families may also make them more visible and therefore more vulnerable.

Summary

The attitudes of the study children toward their blackness was measured by two statements made by the parents. The first, in response to a question in the initial interview, described whether the child was uncomfortable about the differences between his appearance and that of the rest of the family. The second, describing his attitude toward his black heritage, was made in the second interview.

Discomfort about appearance occurred significantly more often in the darkest children, in those whose parents had a strong pro-black orientation, in those whose parents had the most initial reservations about the adoption, and in those whose mothers were relatively young.

Positive attitudes toward black heritage were more likely to be found in homes where the father was a professional, where contact with relatives was frequent, and where the parents' orientation toward race was positive. Children were more likely to be reported as having negative feelings if placed between the ages of 6 and 11 months, but a disproportionately large proportion of these children were fair or light brown.

The child's experience of racial cruelty presented problems in analysis, since it is an ambiguous variable, difficult to place in an analytic scheme. It is also influenced by the sensitivity of the parents to racial issues and by the child's appearance. The trends discerned in the analysis suggested that significantly more such experiences are perceived by parents of girls, by parents living in communities with a nonwhite population of less than 5%, and by families with three or more adopted children.

Chapter 10

A TYPOLOGY OF WHITE FAMILIES WHO ADOPT BLACK CHILDREN

Parents in the study sample are, as noted in Chapter 2,
relatively well-educated and tend to be in upper middle-class
occupations, with relatively high incomes. They also hold political and social views commonly considered liberal and are aware
of and interested in the black community and its problems. This
pattern is similar to that found in other studies of transracial
adopters and, in any case, would have been anticipated from trends
in the contemporary American social scene.

Even within a generally homogeneous population, however, it
is possible to identify different subgroups of parents who vary
on some key characteristics, whose motivation and strength of
conviction may vary, and who may also vary in the degree of success
they have with their children. Identification of such subgroups
can serve as a corrective against over generalization or stereo-
typing.

One recent study indicated that two types of families, differing in age and in motivation, are present in the larger population of families who adopt transracially. Nutt and Snyder
reported a questionnaire study that described 564 families who
adopted transracially.[1] The characteristics of this sample were

---

1. Thomas E. Nutt and John A. Snyder, Transracial Adoption.
   Offset printing, privately distributed, February 1973.

similar to those in the present study. For his doctoral dissertation, Nutt did an intensive study of 40 families in the Boston area, divided evenly between those who had adopted relatively early (before 1969) and later (1970 or later). The data consisted of detailed descriptions of the adoption process as experienced by these parents. In his discussion of the framework for the analysis of a client-bureaucratic system, Nutt suggested that clients in adoption agencies perceive themselves either as patients or as resources. "Patients" are the traditional adoptive couples who approach the agency for help in solving the problem of infertility, expecting to be evaluated and judged. "Resource" couples are those who are not childless but approach agencies to assist in providing homes for "hard-to-place" children, expecting their workers to serve as a guide to the fulfillment of this objective.[2]

A review of the interview data obtained for this study suggested that there might be a similar typology. To test this possibility, a method of cluster analysis was used[3] in which each respondent is compared with all other respondents on a predetermined series of variables. For each variable, a coefficient of dissimilarity is computed that indicates the percentage of cases that would have to be transferred to the other type to make the two alike.

2. Thomas Nutt, Adopting the "Hard-to-Place": System Change in a Public Service. Unpublished Ph. D. dissertation, Massachusetts Institute of Technology, September 1973, p. 24.

3. Jerrold Rubin and Herman Friedman, A Cluster Analysis and Taxonomy System for Grouping and Classifying Data. New York: IBM Corporation, August 1967.

The 21 variables that appeared most related to the suggested typology were entered into the analysis. They are: child's current age, child's age at placement, geographic region, size of community, percentage of nonwhites in the community, mother's age, number of children in the home, number of other adopted children, race of other adopted children, mother's education, husband's employment, wife's employment, income, church attendance, neighborhood (whether totally white or mixed), reason for adoption, child's appearance, number of black friends, degree of contact with relatives, number of friends, and social-political views of the mother (liberal-conservative).

The analysis indicated that the study population could be divided into two groups whose members showed strong dissimilarities on nine of the 21 variables. These are listed in Table 10-1.

Some of the items in the typology are obviously interrelated, e.g., the larger the community, the greater the proportion of non-whites in the population, and the greater the opportunity to have black friends. Highly educated urban families generally have fewer children. Other variables in the typology are more surprising, such as the fact that the small-towners more frequently adopt other black children than the urbanites.

Although some variables used in developing the typology were not strong enough to be considered part of it, they demonstrated trends that were statistically significant or approached significance.

Table 10-1

Typology of Families Adopting Transracially

Group 1 "The Small-Towners" (N=74)	Group 2 "The Urbanites" (N=51)	Coefficients of Dissimilarity
Live in New England, West North Central States, Canada	East North Central, Pacific Coast	.39
Live in communities with less than 50,000 population	Live in communities of over 50,000	.42
Nonwhite population is less than 5%	Nonwhite population is over 5%	.44
Have four or more children in the home	Have three or fewer children	.31
Other (not study subject) adopted children are black	Other adopted children not black	.48
Mother is not a college graduate	Mother is a college graduate	.41
Mother is not employed	Mother is employed as a professional	.34
Mother attends church regularly	Mother attends church infrequently or never	.34
Four or fewer black friends	Five or more black friends	.34

Appearance of Child

The urbanites were more likely than the small-towners to receive lighter children.

This finding is particularly striking since the two groups did not differ in their expectations about the race of the child at the time of placement. Both had the identical proportion (61%)

of those who expressed no preference. The proportion of small-towners who expressed a preference for a black child (20%) was only slightly higher than the proportion with a similar preference (18%) among the urbanites.

Table 10-2

Appearance of Child and Parental Typology

Child's Appearance	Urbanites (N=51) %	Small-Towners (N=74) %
Fair, no Negroid features	22	12
Fair, Negroid features/light brown, no Negroid features	41	27
Light brown or dark, Negroid features	37	61
Total	100	100

Chi-square = 6.78, 2 df, p < .05

Reason for Adoption

Both groups were equally likely to give social reasons, such as making a home for a child in need or working toward integration. The urbanites were more likely to give, as their major reason for adopting, their inability to have as many children as they wanted. The small-towners were more likely to give other personal or circumstantial reasons, such as wanting to adopt a particular foster child or sibling for a biological child, than were the urbanties. These differences miss statistical significance at the .05 level, but come close enough to suggest a trend in this direction.

Table 10-3

Reason for Adoption and Parental Typology

Reason for Adoption	Urbanites (N=51) %	Small-Towners (N=74) %
Infertility problem	49	31
Social motivation	33	35
Other reasons	18	34
	—	—
Total	100	100

Chi-square = 5.45, 2 df, $p < .07$

Social Attitudes of Mothers

A tendency in the expected direction was the much greater likelihood that the urban mothers would describe themselves as liberal or extremely liberal. Ninety percent of them did so, in contrast to 60% of the small-towners.

Several other variables, not included in the original cluster analysis, also demonstrated differences between the two groups. Certain values and aspects of life-style were different for the two groups, as were some aspects of the adoption experience.

Table 10-4

Social Attitudes of Mother and Parental Typology

Social Attitudes	Urbanites (N=51) %	Small-Towners (N=74) %
Liberal	90	60
Middle-of-road/ conservative	10	40
	—	—
Total	100	100

Chi-square = 12.65, 1 df, $p < .001$

Age of Father

As Table 10-5 indicates, most of the fathers in both groups were in their forties. The urbanites, however, had a higher proportion of fathers under 40, while the small-town group had a higher proportion of those over 50.

Table 10-5

Father's Age and Parental Typology

Age	Urbanites (N=46) %	Small-Towners (N=69) %
Under 40	33	17
40 - 49	56	55
50 and over	11	28
Total	100	100

Chi-square = 6.41, 2 df, p < .05

Academic Aspirations for Children

More of the urbanites, as might be expected, had strong aspirations for academic achievement for their children, expecting all children to go to college. Small-towners were more likely to be characterized by modest aspirations, expecting some children to go to college, but not necessarily all. The proportion of "unaspiring" families was only slightly higher for the small-towners than for the urbanites.

Table 10-6

Aspirations for Children and Parental Typology

Aspirations	Urbanites (N=51) %	Small-Towners (N=74) %
Strong aspirations	61	27
Moderate aspirations	16	43
Not aspiring	23	30
Total	100	100

Chi-square = 16.02, 2 df, p < .001

Social Life

The urbanites more often described themselves as having many friends and visiting them frequently than did the small-towners. Twenty percent of the latter described themselves as relatively isolated, seeing friends less than once a month, in contrast to only 6% of the urbanites.

Table 10-7

Social Life and Parental Typology

Number of Friends	Urbanites (N=51) %	Small-Towners (N=74) %	Frequency of Visiting	Urbanites (N=51) %	Small-Towners (N=74) %
Many	75	46	Once a week or oftener	61	38
Few	25	54	1-3 times monthly	33	42
Total	100	100	Less than once a month	6	20
			Total	100	100

Chi-square = 8.95, 1 df, p < .01

Chi-square = 8.28, 2 df, p < .02

Attitudes Toward Race Issues

Responses to the questionnaire data on attitudes toward blacks indicated that the urbanite mothers, as expected from self-described liberals, were more likely to take a "problack" position than the small-town mothers. The latter were more likely to express uncertainty or mixed feelings.

Table 10-8

Mother's Attitudes Toward Blacks and Parental Typology

Attitudes	Urbanites (N=44) %	Small-Towners (N=68) %
Strongly problack	41	32
Problack	43	30
Uncertain/mixed	16	38
Total	100	100

Chi-square = 6.52, 2 df, p < .04

Adoption Experience

The urbanites, not surprisingly, were more likely to express a preference for children with above-average intelligence. With respect to age, they were more likely to express a preference. The urbanites, as the group with strong preferences, were more likely than the small-towners to report that their expectations had not been matched.

Table 10-9

Adoption Experience and Parental Typology

Intellectual Preference	Urbanites (N=51) %	Small-Towners (N=74) %
No intellectual preference	43	57
Prefer high intelligence	35	16
Prefer average intelligence	22	27
Total	100	100

Chi-square = 6.04, 2 df, p < .05

Age Preference		
No age preference	26	55
Prefer under 18 months	31	18
Prefer over 18 months	43	27
Total	100	100

Chi-square = 11.08, 2 df, p < .01

Matching on Intellectual Level		
No preference	43	57
Preferences matched	24	30
Preferences not matched	33	13
Total	100	100

Chi-square = 7.01, 2 df, p < .03

Perception of Cruelty

Small-town parents were more likely to report that their children had experienced some form of cruelty. The urbanites were more likely to deny knowledge of such experience or to deny that the child had had such experiences.

Table 10-10

Perception of Cruelty and Parental Typology

Cruelty	Urbanites (N=44) %	Small-Towners (N=70) %
Some experience	34	58
Unknown	27	13
No experience	39	29
	—	—
Total	100	100

Chi-square = 7.19, 2 df, p < .03

This relationship may be readily explained by the information in Table 10-2, which demonstrated that small-towners have the more visibly black children, as well as the findings in Chapter 9 that the more visibly black children experience more cruelty. However, additional analysis indicated that, when the children of light appearance are left out of the analysis, the small-towners still tended to report these experiences significantly more often than the urbanites. This is also consistent with the finding reported in the previous chapter that the families in communities with a relatively low nonwhite population reported such episodes more frequently.

Differences: Outcome

Finally, the major question with respect to this typology is whether either group is more successful than the other in rearing black children. On the summary index, 43% of the urbanites had below-average scores, while 37% had above-average. Thirty-eight percent of the small-town families had below-average scores and

42% had above-average. This very slight difference is not statistically significant and it may be said that the two groups do equally well and are equally vulnerable to problems.

The same absence of significant differences was noted on all the specific measures of outcome, with two exceptions. Urban parents reported more symptoms in their children in the first interview than did their small-town counterparts.

Table 10-11

Symptoms Score and Parental Typology

Symptoms	Urbanites (N=51) %	Small-Towners (N=74) %
Moderate/high	61	37
Minimal/none	39	63
Total	100	100

Chi-square = 7.17, 1 df, p < .01

It is possible that urban mothers, with more education and fewer children, were more sensitive or more observant where health matters were concerned. It is also possible that more positive relations with the interviewers, noted in Chapter 7, made it easier for them to acknowledge symptoms than it was for the small-towners. In any case, the difference was not present at Time 2.

At Time 1, when the interviewer ratings were focused on family relationships, they demonstrated a tendency to perceive the small-town mothers as relatively less warm than the urbanites. This difference, however, misses statistical significance. At Time 2, when the ratings were focused on the family's ability to deal with the racial aspects of the adoption, the interviewers favored the urbanites even more strongly and produced a difference that is statistically significant.

Table 10-12

Interviewer Ratings and Parental Typology

Time 1 Rating	Urbanites (N=51) %	Small-Towners (N=74) %
Not warm	18	35
Warm	31	27
Very warm	51	38
	___	___
Total	100	100

Chi-square = 4.70, 2 df, $p < .10$

Time 2 Rating	(N=44)	(N=70)
Somewhat negative	16	44
Positive	32	23
Very positive	52	33
	___	___
Total	100	100

Chi-square = 9.88, 2 df, $p < .001$

This relationship again raises the question of interviewer bias. Since the interviewers were themselves middle-class professionals, were they more likely to identify with, and see in a more positive light, people like themselves? Whatever the degree of bias, the difference between the two assessments suggests that interviewers were much more skeptical of the small-towners' ability to handle the specifically racial issues in these adoptions than they were of the urbanites' ability.

Summary

Through the method of cluster analysis, two subgroups of trans-racial adopters were identified. The larger group consisted of families who lived in small towns with few nonwhites in the population, and who had four or more children. The mother was not a college graduate, not employed, and attended church regularly. These families had relatively few black friends, but their adopted children other than the study subject tended to be black. The smaller group lived in large cities with larger nonwhite populations and had families with three of fewer children. The mother was a college graduate, employed as a professional. These families rarely or never attended church. They tended to have many black friends, but other adopted children tended to be white.

Further analysis showed other significant differences between the groups. Fathers in the urban group tended to be younger. The urban families tended to have more friends, whom they saw more frequently. They had stronger academic aspirations for their children. Urban mothers were more likely to describe themselves as liberals and to maintain a strongly problack position on racial issues. The urban families were more likely to give infertility as a reason for adoption than the small-towners. They were more likely to prefer children of high intelligence, to have an age preference, and to report that their preferences had not been matched. The urbanites were more likely to receive light children than the small-town families, despite the fact that they did not express a preference in this direction. They were less likely to report that their children had experienced cruelty than the small-town families.

On the summary index scores measuring the successful adjustment of the child, both groups did equally well. Of the specific measures of success, only two differentiated between the two groups. The urban families tended to report more symptoms in their children than did the small-town families. On the other hand, they were more favorably rated by the interviewers, particularly on the racial aspects of the adoption.

The identification of this typology suggests that there are at least two groups of families willing and able to undertake a transracial adoption, but these groups do not fit the patient-resource person typology suggested by Nutt. The sources of their motivation may be different; the small-towners may be basing their actions on religious beliefs and the urban families on secular liberalism, but the capacity for both to be parents to the children they adopt seems equally good. If the interviewers' ratings are valid, one may infer that the small-town families need more help with the racial aspects of the adoption, but in the overall assessment they are as successful as the urban families.

Chapter 11

SUMMARY AND DISCUSSION

Transracial adoptive placements have been made by agencies
over the last two decades, as the needs of black children for
permanent homes became increasingly visible. Since the number
of black families attracted by agencies trying to place black
adoptive children in permanent homes was not sufficient to the
need, some agencies dropped the requirement for racial matching
and began to place children across racial lines. A number of
social changes--particularly the decrease in white adoptable
children and public reaction to the population explosion--rein-
forced this trend, and the number of transracial placements grew
accordingly.

This study was undertaken by the Child Welfare League in response to the need for data about the outcome of transracial
adoptions, when the trend toward such placements was growing.
About the time the study was initiated, this practice became
openly controversial in the social work community as the National
Association of Black Social Workers issued a strong statement in
opposition to the practice. The precise effect of this position
on adoption practice is difficult to assess, as is the influence
of the League's reiterating its position that inracial placement
is preferable. It is known that most agencies that pioneered
in transracial adoption have made fewer such placements of late,

while some agencies where such placements had not been made
earlier have initiated the practice despite less encouragement
of it.

The study was completed as planned and, now that its findings have been reported, their implications for adoption practice
have to be considered. Prior to this discussion, the principal
findings are summarized.

Study Design

The study was directed to black children who were at least
6 years old, who had been in white adoptive homes for at least 3
years. Parents were interviewed at the point of selection for
participation in this study and interviewed again a year later
to assess the stability of the picture obtained at the first
interview. The sample was drawn from social agencies in communities where relatively large numbers of transracial adoptions
had been made. Twenty-five agencies identified 227 families
eligible for the study. Of these, 125 (55%) were finally interviewed. Of those who were not interviewed, most could not be
located or did not return the consent form to the agency.

Instruments used in the first period of data collection
include a joint parent interview, individual interviews with each
parent, questionnaires completed by each parent, and the California Test of Personality for the child. The parent questionnaire included two measures derived from previous studies, the
Weinstein Scale of Well-Being and scales from the Missouri Chil-

dren's Behavior Checklist. . Parents were asked for permission to contact the child's teacher, and when this was given the teacher was sent a one-page form asking for her or his judgment of the child's academic work and classroom behavior. At the second contact, parents were interviewed jointly and again asked to complete a questionnaire separately. At the end of both the first and second interviews, the social workers who served as interviewers rated various aspects of the family's and child's adjustment, as well as the parents' ability to handle the racial aspects of the adoption.

Data collected through these instruments covered a wide range of topics. With respect to the family, these included descriptions of the general family situation, the neighborhood, the family's leisure activity, the parents' general social attitudes, their attitudes on racial issues, and their contacts with blacks and black culture. Their recall of the adoption experience, their general satisfaction or dissatisfaction with the adoption, the reactions of family and friends to the adoption, the parents' activities with the child, their attitudes toward child rearing, their openness to "waiting" children were explored. A major focus was, of course, the study child's behavior and adjustment, with attention given to her or his racial awareness and sense of identity.

The data obtained were coded for machine processing. Harvard Data-Text programs for correlations, cross-tabulation and regression analysis were used. Indices were developed to measure

a variety of aspects of the child's adjustment and the parents'

feelings about the adoption considered relevant to the success

of transracial adoption. A series of independent variables, in-

cluding demographic characteristics of the child, the family and

the community, as well as those reflecting the family's life-style,

adoption experience, and attitudes toward blacks, were then re-

lated to each of the outcome measures. Regression analysis was

used to assess the relative influence of significant variables

on the various measures of outcome. A cluster analysis was also

carried out, dividing the adoptive families into two general

types.

Description of the Sample

The Children

The study children included 61 girls and 64 boys with a

median age of 8.8 years, in their adoptive homes a median of

7.2 years. They were older at placement than most adopted chil-

dren. Most were described as having fair or light brown skin

coloring and some Negroid features, but only slightly more than

half were "obviously" black, according to their parents.

Most children were in a school grade appropriate for their

ages, taught by predominantly white teachers and with no other

black children in the class. Most were doing average or above-

average work in school, according to their parents, and teacher

ratings also indicated that most were doing as well as or better than their peers in the classroom. Most were reported to be in good health and symptom-free. Most were also getting along well with other children, having close friends and good relationships with siblings, even though about half were reported to have experienced some form of social cruelty. Most were receiving some form of religious training and participating in organized recreational activities.

The study children scored higher on the personal adjustment measures of the California Test of Personality than on the social adjustment measures. They compared well on the total adjustment scores with the sample of white adopted children in a comparable study.

Families

Nearly all study children were living with both adopted parents in a nuclear family. Most parents were in their thirties at the time of the adoption and most had been married between five and 14 years. Most had biological children at the time of placement, and about a third had already adopted one or more other children. By the time of followup, a third had adopted other black children.

Most of the adoptive parents were college graduates. The fathers were usually professionals. The median family income was $15,700. Most of these families lived in communities with populations of 50,000 or less, in totally or predominantly white neighborhoods, among neighbors whom slightly over half described

as "fairly conservative" but nevertheless relatively accepting
of black families living in their neighborhoods. Parents tended
to describe themselves as liberal. Nearly all reported a religious affiliation, and most of the affiliated attended church.
Most had relatives living in the area, and maintained contact
with them.

Four-fifths of the families reported having black friends
or acquaintances. Most families reported that their children
were aware of their black parentage. Most parents attached importance to their child's knowledge of his background, and most
had discussed the child's racial background with him. Most
parents were judged by the interviewers as able to handle race-
related problems. Most reported having read books written by or
about blacks, but other activities directed toward awareness of
black heritage were less frequently reported. Most parents
maintained contact with other friends who adopted transracially.
Most agreed that it was important for the child to have pride in
his heritage and were strongly sympathetic to the problems of
blacks in society. There was less agreement about whether the
problems of rearing a black child were any different from those
of rearing any other child.

The Adoption Experience

Families were fairly evenly divided between those who gave
infertility as the reason for adoption, those who gave social
reasons such as a concern for children without homes, and those

who adopted as a result of circumstance, such as an attachment
to a foster child. Most had no racial preference. Reasons for
deciding to adopt transracially were usually social in nature,
e.g., the desire to provide a home for a hard-to-place child.
Although most denied any reservations about their ability to
adopt transracially, nearly half admitted some concern about the
extended family's reaction. Slightly over half, however, reported that relatives were supportive from the beginning. Most dis-
approving relatives were reported to have changed their attitudes
once the adoption took place.

Most of these parents indicated that they would have adopted
a child of any racial background. They were less open to the
possibility of adopting an older, handicapped or retarded child.
Almost half had no age preference, but those who had one tended
to want children between 3 months and 3 years old. Two-thirds
expressed an intellectual preference, evenly divided between
those who preferred average intelligence and those who preferred above-average. Of these, half indicated that their expectations had been met. Usually their preferences had been explored by the worker.

Most families were satisfied with the information given
them about their children, although a substantial minority felt
they were not well informed about the child's health and his
experiences prior to placement.

Most parents described their experience in rearing the study child as extremely satisfying and felt that the adoption had turned out as well as or better than they expected. Most parents reported that their marriages were happier and expressed satisfaction in the companionship given by the child and the opportunity to express their love for children. Nearly all parents were certain that the adoption of racially mixed children by either white or black families should be encouraged, but there were more reservations about adoption of wholly white or black children across racial lines.

Correlates of Success

"Success"

The relative success of these adoptions was assessed by a set of 15 measures that included test scores, teacher evaluations, interviewer ratings, and indices developed from different types of data supplied by the parents. The scores on these measures were combined in a single score to measure overall success. Data on the cases with low scores were reviewed and a combined judgment made as to which of these adoptions could be considered to be in serious difficulty. Twenty-seven of the 125 adoptions were included in this group, which gives the sample a success rate of 77%. This rate is approximately the same as that of other studies that have examined conventional white infant adoption, as well as those concerned with the adoption of older children and other racial groups.

An examination of the relationship between the summary
score and variables describing the family and child indicates
only two statistically significant relationships. Children perceived by their parents as obviously black were more likely to
have higher summary scores than those whose blackness was perceived as not obvious. Children in the largest family units
(five or more children) were also likely to have higher scores
than those in smaller units. No other characteristic--demograph-
ic or attitudinal--used in this study predicted overall success.

When the specific measures of success were analyzed in relation to the other success measures, most showed a significant
relationship to some of the others. However, those that reflected the child's attitude toward being black showed few relationships to the general measures of the child's well-being.

When each of the measures of success was examined in relation to the independent variables describing the child and the
family, different patterns emerged for different success measures.
That is, some variables predicted some forms of success but not
others. In no case was the relationship between the descriptive
variable and any form of outcome so strong that the variable
could be regarded as highly predictive. But relationships that
occur more often than can be explained by chance are at least
suggestive of factors relevant to success, and have therefore
been reported. When these are grouped by content, the following

patterns emerged.

Influential Variables Describing the Child

Girls were less aggressive than boys, freer of neurotic symptoms, and had better evaluations from their teachers.

Children over 12 years old were freer of neurotic symptoms, but children under 10 were freer of physical symptoms. Age at placement was unrelated to any form of success, except for an indication that those placed between 6 and 11 months, who tended to be lighter than others, were more likely to have negative feelings about their black heritage than other children. Children in placement over 5 years had higher personal and social adjustment scores on the California Test of Personality. They also received better evaluations from their teachers.

Children with brown skin or some Negroid features were likely to be freer of inhibitions than children at either extreme of appearance, the very light and the very dark. The darkest children were the ones most likely to be perceived as uncomfortable about the difference in their appearance from that of the family. Children described as obviously black were more likely to be free of physical symptoms.

Influential Variables Describing the Family

Children were more likely to be free of neurotic symptoms and of discomfort about their appearance when their mothers were over 40 at the time of followup.

Children entering a two-sibling family at the time of adoption were more likely to have difficulty in sibling relations than others. The greater the number of children currently living in the home, the greater the likelihood that the child would be free of neurotic symptoms.

Children of parents married 10 to 14 years had better ratings from their teachers than did others.

Symptoms were less frequently reported by mothers whose education was limited to high school. Families with better-educated mothers, on the other hand, received higher ratings from interviewers on their ability to handle the racial issues involved in the adoption.

Children of fathers who are professionals were more often reported as having good relationships with other children and as having positive attitudes toward their black heritage.

Children in families with a middle-range income for this population ($15-19,000) had better social adjustment scores than those in families with lower or higher incomes.

Children in Protestant or Catholic families had better personal adjustment scores than those with other affiliations or the unaffiliated.

It may be worth noting that whether the mother was employed or the type of employment she was engaged in bore no relation to any form of success.

Influential Variables Related to the Adoption Experience

Children of parents who gave infertility as the reason for adoption were less likely to have low scores on social adjustment. These families also received higher ratings on family relations from the interviewers than did others. Families who gave social reasons for adopting transracially reported fewer symptoms in their children.

Children with low teacher ratings tended to have parents who had expressed a preferance for children with average intelligence at the time of adoption. Parents whose intellectual expectations were not matched had children with more neurotic symptoms and higher inhibition scores.

Parents who were relatively free of reservations at the time of the adoption decision reported less discomfort in their children about differences in appearance.

Parents who were satisfied with the service they had received from the agency had children with lower aggression scores, had better ratings from the interviewers on their ability to handle racial issues, and were more likely to be generally satisfied with the adoption.

Mothers who were ambivalent about the adoption of a handicapped child had children with low social adjustment and high aggression scores. Mothers who were open to the adoption of a handicapped child were more likely to be favorably rated on their ability to handle racial issues and to be satisfied with the adoption of the study child.

Fathers who were ambivalent about the adoption of a handicapped child were more likely to report that their children had
problems in their relations with other children.

Parents who had doubts about the validity of totally transracial adoption had children with relatively high inhibition
scores and a high frequency of symptoms.

Families who had three or more adopted children were more
likely to report experience of cruelty.

It is worth noting that in the area of adoption experience,
the presence of biological children, the race of other adopted
children, whether the parents already had an adopted child at
the time of study child's adoption, and their initial age or race
preference had no relation to any measures of success.

Influential Variables Affecting Familial Life-style

Families who regularly attended church drew higher ratings
from the interviewers on their ability to handle racial issues
than those who did not.

Families whose social contacts were relatively infrequent
reported better sibling relations than others.

Families in frequent contact with relatives reported greater
satisfaction with the adoption and more positive attitudes on the
part of the children toward their black heritage.

Mothers with a disciplinary approach that is neither very
strict nor very permissive received more positive ratings from

the interviewers on family relations. Fathers with similar middle-range scores on permissiveness were more likely to have children with high aggression scores.

In this area, it may be noted that aspirations for academic achievement have no bearing on any form of "success."

Influential Variables Reflecting Attitudes Toward Race

The stronger the parents' orientation toward race, as measured by a combination of activities and attitudes, the greater the likelihood of a positive attitude on the part of the child toward his heritage.

Mothers whose attitudes toward blacks as expressed in questionnaire responses were relatively less favorable, were less likely to report problems in sibling relationships. Fathers with a moderately problack attitude were more likely to report children who were symptom-free. When both parents were strongly "problack," they were more likely to report that the study child had some discomfort about appearance and the child was more likely to have a relatively high aggression score.

Children reported by their parents as having experienced some form of social cruelty were also reported to be relatively free of symptoms and to have good relations with other children.

Community Characteristics

Families living in Canada and New England tended to be less favorably evaluated by interviewers than those living elsewhere.

Children living in communities of over 250,000 had better social adjustment scores, and fewer episodes of cruelty were reported by the parents. Families living in neighborhoods that were not totally white reported a greater degree of satisfaction with the adoption.

Types of Adoptive Parents

Although the sample of adoptive families was generally homogeneous, two subtypes of families were discerned through the method of cluster analysis. The larger group--the "small-towners"--were families living in smaller cities with few nonwhites in the population. They tended to have relatively large families, with mothers who were not college graduates and not employed. They attended church regularly. They had relatively few black friends, but their adopted children other than study subjects tended to be black.

The smaller group, or "urbanites," lived in larger cities with larger nonwhite populations and had fewer children. The mother was a college graduate, employed in a professional occupation. These families rarely or never attended church. They tended to have many black friends, but their other adopted children tended to be white.

These two groups tended to differ in other ways as well. Fathers in the urbanite group tended to be younger. Their families also tended to have more friends and to have stronger academic aspirations for their children. The urban mothers were more likely to describe themselves as liberals and to maintain a strong problack position. They were also more likely to prefer children of high intelligence, to have an age preference, and to report that their preferences had not been matched. They were more likely to receive relatively light children, though they did not express a preference in this direction. They were less likely to report that their children had experienced cruelty than the small-towners.

Both groups did equally well on the overall measure of successful adjustment. On the specific measures, the urban families reported more symptoms in their children but were also more favorably evaluated by the interviewers, particularly on their ability to handle the racial aspects of the adoption.

Overview

In reviewing the findings related to specific focus of outcome, one may note that only six variables influence more than one form of outcome, do so in a way that is consistent, and do not raise questions of circularity or present other problems of interpretation. One may then say that the following factors, in addition to the parents' ability to acknowledge the blackness of their child and the size of the family, tend to predict a somewhat greater degree of success in a transracial adoption:

1. The adoptee is a girl.

2. The adoptee has been in placement at least 5 years.

3. The adoptive father is in a professional occupation.

4. An infertility problem provided the initial motivation for adoption.

5. The adoptive family has frequent contact with relatives.

6. The agency met the family's preference with respect to the child's intellectual level.

Discussion

Before considering the practice implications of these findings, several limitations in the study should be noted. The sample consists of only 125 cases, although the study cases were drawn from 25 agencies in a diversity of communities. The participant families were necessarily volunteers. Most of the instruments used were developed specifically for this study, and there is no way of testing their reliability or validity. Furthermore, the adoptive placements were made on the average almost 10 years ago, when the social scene was different from today's. There is really no way to judge how these facts affect the relevance of the findings.

Another limitation of a somewhat different order is that the children in the sample include only a relatively small group who have reached adolescence.

Most of the study children were in the early school years, a period in which a sense of identity along racial lines and a knowledge of the meaning of race in the larger society are just beginning to develop. As was noted earlier, it is impossible, without a followup study, to say just how the children's attitudes toward blackness will change by the time they reach adolescence and early adulthood. Thus it was not possible to give a definitive answer to the question whether white adoptive parents can deal successfully with the problem of racial identity. The only statement that can be made is that the evidence of this study indicates that racial identity is not reported as a major problem by the parents, knowing that the evidence we have is influenced by the degree of the parents' openness and interest in this area to begin with. One can say that, in terms of general well-being, the large majority of the children in this sample were doing well and that the degree of success of this form of adoption compared favorably with that of other types of adoption that have been studied.

This key finding of a high degree of general success, taken together with similar findings in other studies of atypical adoptions, indicates that the trend of the last decade toward greater flexibility in the acceptance of adoptive applicants is justified by the results. A case cannot be made for the perpetuation of the older system, which limited adoption to infertile couples seeking an infant who would take the place of the biological child they were unable to have, and left the children who did not meet this need in the foster care system.

If the indications are that the adoption system can be successfully opened up to meet needs that in the past were assumed to be beyond its capacities, the next question that arises is whether the need for adoptive placement for black children is as great at it was when the practice of transracial placement began.

Efforts were made to recruit more black adoptive homes before transracial adoptions were made, and continued after they
became increasingly common. The drive to recruit more black
homes was reinforced by the strong opposition of some black
social workers to transracial placement. The latter contended
that, with appropriate effort on the part of black professionals
and their agencies, and with the use of media based in the black
community, the need for adoptive homes could be met.

Again, there is little precise data to assess the impact of
such efforts either before or after the militant position was
taken. The major source of information on national adoption
trends is the Child Welfare League's semiannual report, in which
49 voluntary and 18 public agencies participate. Its latest report states that "the recent stability of nonwhite homes is somewhat discouraging: it has varied from 59 to 67 homes per 100 children over the past 2 years, even lower than during the three
earliest periods of the series (begun in 1971), when it ranged between 74 and 85. Recruitment of nonwhite homes has a long way to
go to match or exceed the number of nonwhite children accepted."[1]

In the absense of strong evidence to the contrary, one must
infer that the need for permanent homes for black children has
not been met despite active efforts to recruit black homes. The
findings of this study are therefore still relevant to the prob-

1. CWLA Adoption Statistics--January-June '74, Compared With
   July-December '73 Summary of Findings. Child Welfare League
   of America, October 1974 (mimeographed).

-235-

lems of contemporary adoption practice and not, as one might have
expected a few years ago, a description of a short-lived deviation.
If transracial adoptions are generally successful and the need
still there, it is a question whether this practice should be
discontinued.

The finding that children perceived by their parents as obviously black do better than those described as not obviously
black also has some important implications. This indicates that
the less-well "matched" children do better than the better "matched,"
for whom denial of difference is easier. This in turn may mean
that parents who acknowledge openly the child's difference may
also have the ego strength to deal competently with the problems
of child rearing in general. Conversely, parents who deny the
child's difference may also tend to use this defense mechanism
more generally and with negative consequences. The few cases of
total denial noted in the earlier chapters indicate the extreme
ways in which this defense can be used.

However, this does not mean that other dimensions in matching are not important. As the findings indicated, the fact that
the child did not match the intellectual expectation of the parents, whether for average or above-average intelligence, was
associated with more neurotic symptoms and less favorable test
scores on inhibition. Matching for intelligence is, of course,
more difficult and hazardous than matching for appearance, and
one cannot expect agencies to be able to control the process

completely. Nevertheless, the findings imply that failures in this area have more significant consequences than the "unmatched" appearance.

Another finding with implications for practice is the indication that children in placement less than 5 years had lower personal and social adjustment scores on the California Test of Personality and lower evaluations from their teachers. This suggests that, although the long-range expectation for success is good, the adjustment process in these adoptions may be relatively long and require support, reinforcing the importance of continuing agency service after legal adoption.

The typology of adoptive parents described in the analysis also carries some implications for recruitment. The tendency of parents in transracial adoptions to be liberal, well-educated, and independent in their thinking, noted in this and other studies, might imply that such adoptions should be undertaken only by persons with these characteristics. In the contemporary American social scene, it is easy to see the country as polarized between those who are liberal, educated, "anti-Establishment," responsive to experiments in life-style, on the one hand, and the conservative, conventional, less-educated and less-urban "middle Americans," and to regard transracial adoption as appropriate only for the former. The findings in relation to the typology imply that the country is not so polarized as such stereotypes imply. It is possible to adhere to a relatively conventional "middle-American" life-style, yet be relatively free of prejudices in the area of race and have something to offer children whose racial background is different. It may be, as some of the findings have indicated, that the small-town parents needed more help in some areas than did the more urban parents, but the relative success of the adoptions in the sample was closely comparable for the small-towners and the urbanites.

Some of the findings suggest that problems of bias are as likely to be found with the professionals in adoption as with their clients, if not more so. In this regard, the finding that the urban families received lighter children than the small-town families, even though they did not express a preference in this direction, is disturbing. It brings to mind the findings of two earlier adoption studies,[2] which indicated that workers tended to match parents of higher socioeconomic status with "normal" children, whereas parents of lower or marginal status were given "deviant" children, so that "better" children went to "better" families. One wonders, then, whether the light-skinned child in a transracial adoption is seen as a "better" baby to be placed with the "better" family. Both the dictates of common sense and the findings in this study indicate that if black children are to be adopted by families in communities with few nonwhites, they should be the lighter children who will not be conspicious in the

---

2. Alfred Kadushin, "A Study of Adoptive Parents of Hard-to-Place Children," Social Casework, Vol. 43, No. 5 (May 1962), p. 227. Henry S. Maas, "The Successful Adoptive Parent Applicant," Social Work, Vol. 5, No. 1 (Jan. 1950), p. 14.

community, while the more urban families could take darker children who would not be conspicuous in communities with a greater degree of heterogeneity. Yet the reverse is what actually happened. One is mindful of the fact that these placements were made in the fifties and the early sixties, and one cannot say whether such biases may have been modified later. Nevertheless, such findings indicate that the specter of white middle-class bias in social work practice has not been laid, and that there is a continuing need for critical self-examination in this area.

A black home for every black child has not as yet become a reality, despite vigorous recruitment efforts, beginning availability of adoption subsidy, and modification of agency procedures in evaluating adoptive applicants. Such efforts should unquestionably be intensified, since no one disputes the preferability of a black home for a black child. Until that objective is reached, society is left with a choice between adoption of some black children by white parents and having these children grow up without the continuity and security of a family of their own. The apparent success of the large majority of adoptions in this study suggests that we should not reject the alternative of adoption of black children by white parents.